Dodging Bullets, Shooting Back

DODGING BULLETS, SHOOTING BACK

SURVIVING ON THE CORPORATE BATTLEFIELD

Harry R. Rozakis

ISBN: 151880411X
ISBN 13: 9781518804113

For Diane

CONTENTS

INTRODUCTION

The Best Time to Dodge a Bullet

The best time to dodge a bullet is before
the gun is in the shooter's hand!
—Harry Rozakis

Ll over the world in large corporations and small businesses, from the halls of government to your local DMV, there are bodies scattered about with their professional lives shot out from under them because of the failure to heed this advice. There are those individuals who have been stopped dead in their tracks, others fatally wounded, some licking their wounds, and some simply grazed. What they all have in common is that someone, some group, or in some cases some*thing* has taken a shot at them and has hit its mark. Some failed to see the bullets heading for them, and others saw them too late, while still others had no clue on how to dodge a bullet. The smart ones—and in some cases the lucky ones—were not only able to dodge the bullet but were able to fire back. This is a book about learning how to dodge those bullets and how to fire back.

In many instances, people who take a bullet fundamentally don't recognize that someone had their sights set on them. They are so preoccupied with the goings on in their job and their daily lives that they never see that the world around them is changing and that those changes will make them a target for all kinds of attacks. Some have their faces so buried in their computers or on their mobile devices that they are not paying attention. Then there are those people, though few in number, who believe they are invulnerable to bullets; they believe their exceptional job performance, their tenure with the company, or in some cases their insignificance to the company make them not only unlikely targets but ones impervious to attack. Occasionally, these individuals are those who maintain a high stature within an organization: CEOs, COOs, CFOs, and presidents whose hubris and arrogance convince them of their own invulnerability. Then there are those situations where individuals simply lack the astuteness and ability to identify where the bullets are coming from or the types of weapons being fired. It's just not part of their tool case.

It is not uncommon for employees or even leaders to not be able to comprehend—or for that matter, even believe—the reality that they are being shot at, so they stand in disbelief as the bullets speed toward them. This is a common occurrence, and it is why every day in businesses around the world bodies fall *"not with a bang but a whimper."* In some instances, there are mass shootings; in others moments, individuals fall one at a time. But make no mistake, if you are living in the real world, the bullets are always flying.

Amid the rubble of tattered bodies and damaged careers, there are those individuals who like the mythological phoenix are able rise again and live to fight another day. These individuals, though few and far between, have not only come to learn how to identify where the bullets come from, but more importantly, they've learned how to identify who the shooters are. If you can identify the shooter(s), you can take action. Not only can you dodge bullets and run for cover, but you can position yourself to shoot back. If you are particularly adept, you may be able to disarm the shooter before he or she has even picked up the gun. It is rare that shooting back will take out your adversary completely, but it will assuredly make the shooter(s) rethink who they are shooting at and possibly hold their fire until a more equitable arrangement can be worked out.

Who are these shooters anyhow? This is a critical question, because if you don't know what to look for, how are you ever going to dodge a bullet? What this book does is provide the characteristics of the various sources of the bullets and identify the traits of the respective individuals who are firing. It takes a serious look at their process of loading their weapons and taking aim at their respective target. It gives the reader a means for avoiding becoming a target, or at least protects you from being hit once the bullets start flying.

Shooters come in many shapes and sizes. They represent every race, religion, culture, national origin, and gender. Sometimes they are not even human. Some attempt to disguise themselves. Some are actually overt with respect to their intentions. Their weapons of choice vary. There is, however, always one certainty, and that is once they pick up their weapon, they are shooting to kill. In some instances, they shoot indiscriminately and couldn't care less about collateral damage. At times the shooters can even be suicidal. The fact is, shooters exist in every type of business, and they do their job without conscience and in a majority of the cases without malice. There are some shooters who actually take pleasure in a "kill," and those who feign deep remorse. However, if you are on the receiving side of their intentions, what they feel becomes totally irrelevant. Quite simply, they're on a hunt, and you, your team, or your business is their prey.

As you move through the chapters of this book, you will come across an array of armed individuals. You will meet the *hired gun*, who always knows his target and is relentless in achieving his goal. You will meet the *sniper*, who sits in wait. She watches as you move about believing you are safe, only to end your professional life with blinding speed as she keeps herself deep within the shadows. For the *gunslinger*, it is nothing more than target practice. You may even know who this person is; you just never expected him or her to aim their gun at you. When the target is powerful or capable of retaliation, a *posse* may be formed to ensure the target is outgunned. At other times, there may simply be a new *marshal* in town who imposes his own rules and shoots first and asks questions later.

Not all people, however, fall victim to a direct shot fired by an identifiable shooter. *Friendly fire* can often be a devastating blow because it is what the victim least expects and can be extremely difficult to identify. *Collateral damage* falls into this category to a degree. If the workplace has become a battleground, then one must be alert to the possibility of collateral damage, but when there seems to be a peaceful environment, unexpected shootings could result in significant damages. Collateral damage can also occur during *war games*. War games arise during M&A (merger and acquisition) activities, joint ventures, and divestitures. They can be extremely bloody and carry with them considerable collateral damage.

Now, there are a few who will read this book who are caught up in political correctness and feel that the metaphors I am using and the entire concept of dodging bullets and shooting back is inappropriate in some way. To those who feel that way, I say "lighten up" or don't read the book, because believe it or not, your political correctness has already made you a target.

The expression "I dodged a bullet" has been around for a long time and was never meant to offend anyone. It's just a way of saying there are a lot of dangers in the corporate world and one need always be alert. With that in mind, this book is being written with a touch of "tongue in cheek" humor, an ounce of critical thinking, and an overwhelming dose of reality. And who knows, maybe by writing this disclaimer I've just dodged my first bullet.

In the coming pages, we will identify those who fire the bullets and the kinds of weapons they use. There characteristics and trademarks will be identified, along with their modus operandi for doing what they do. Being able to understand each of these categories of shooters will take you a long way toward recognizing them and assuring that their sights will never be aimed at you. The book also provides some actions you can take to ensure that not only can you dodge anything that's fired in your direction but you can avoid having to dodge bullets at all.

Shooting back takes a far greater effort than dodging bullets. Shooting back can be extremely costly depending on the approach and can also paint a bigger target on a person's back than originally existed. Shooting back is never a knee-jerk reaction; it is a planned, well-thought-out strategy with specific results intended and a clearly defined target.

SECTION I

SHOOTERS—WHAT YOU SHOULD KNOW

> *I couldn't do that. Could you do that? Why can they do it? Who are those guys?*
> —ROBERT REDFORD AS BUTCH CASSIDY, FROM THE MOVIE BUTCH CASSIDY AND THE SUNDANCE KID

CHAPTER 1

BAD GUYS DON'T ALWAYS WEAR BLACK

Know first who you are; then adorn yourself accordingly.
—EURIPIDES

If you believe you may be a target and you begin looking for the guy in the black hat, you're already dead. In the corporate world and even in the world of small business and government, bad guys never wear black. The guy in the pinstriped suit can as easily be your friend as he can be the hired gun paid to take you out. The colleague in blue jeans might be carrying a side arm or he might just be the guy who likes to wear blue jeans. The person in the white smock is not always a physician or a lab tech, and the pretty woman in the tight-fitting dress is not always just eye candy for drooling chauvinistic men. The good-looking, smooth-talking guy isn't always trying to hit on you, and his end game isn't always to get you in bed.

Those of us who go back far enough may remember the adage "dress for success." Dressing for success no longer means wearing a Hickey Freeman suit, custom-made white shirt, Donna Karin pants outfit, Zegna ties, and Gucci shoes. Not every man at IBM wears a white shirt anymore, nor does every woman wear a dress. Not every banker wears a tie, and not every construction boss wears the grit of the jobsite. The suit no longer "makes the man," and dressing sexy (for the most part) no longer advances your career (except maybe in Washington, DC). Attire no longer goes hand and hand with one's ambition, and attire definitely doesn't help you recognize the shooters from the nonshooters. Clothes don't tell you who prospective or possible shooters are, and they clearly don't have bull's-eyes on them to tell you who's going to be shot. A slick suit or a power pantsuit no longer gives shooters away. "Power players" today can be the guys in blue jeans and the black T-shirt, or the women in a casual skirt and running shoes. They can be the guy who just left the gym, or the woman on her way to a Bikram yoga class. Remember, however, that the person taking aim is not necessarily a "power player," so attire ends up having no role at all in terms of identifying shooters. They could be in a nurse's uniform, overalls, or dressed in religious attire. The fact is, you just don't know. If you believe all the stories about congress, you'd believe that shots have even been taken by those in the congressional sauna with nothing but a towel on and possibly nothing at all. I don't think any of us want to think about the functional and dysfunctional weapons that have passed through the congressional sauna.

Having said that clothes are not a means to identify shooters is accurate, but clothes can be a clue in some instances. A new suit, a new dress, a pair of clean sneakers, or a change in mode of dress can be a tip-off when combined with other warning signs. Over my career, I have seen these kinds of things time and time again. I have seen CFOs and COOs who are normally casually dressed guys in a company suddenly show up in a Brioni suit when board members show up for a "special" meeting with the company's CEO: guys who have been hungry for the CEO's job unconsciously reflecting their ambitions through their style of dress. There have been lab guys who usually show up in jeans and a lab coat suddenly wearing neat khakis and a dress shirt when they know the CTO or VP of technology's job is on the line. Or consider a guy showing up for his warehouse job in a brand-new set of jeans, a Polo shirt, cleaned and shined boots, and a new baseball cap when the foreman's job has been put on the line. Couple these signs with changes in behavior, whispers in the corner, or all-out statements like "I could do that guy's job better," and the change of attire immediately becomes a warning sign.

We live in a new world where black and white hats are not the criteria for identifying good and bad. Some might say that world is now gray or, as some have said, "orange is the new black," and distinguishing the good from the bad is difficult because everyone is a little good and a little bad. Good and bad, however, is not about which end of the gun barrel you stand on. I would argue that our world is not gray but rather has become a kaleidoscope of colors. Bad guys wear pink...and green and turquoise...and red, white, and blue. Good guys may wear the same exact colors. The point is that neither good nor bad are wearing white and black hats. They're the folks at the football games with the multicolored hair and a clown outfit. The thing with clowns: some are like the good-natured Bozo or Ronald McDonald, whereas others are like the one from Stephen King's *It*.

CHAPTER 2

THE HIRED GUN: "HAVE GUN, WILL TRAVEL"

An empty gun can tell a man a lot of things.
—*RICHARD BOONE AS PALADIN IN HAVE GUN—WILL TRAVEL,*
"THE GREAT MOJAVE CHASE," SEASON 1, EPISODE 3, 1957

If you're a baby boomer, you probably remember the old western starring Richard Boone called *Have Gun—Will Travel*. For those who are not familiar with it, in this fifties western show, Richard Boone played the role of Paladin, a hired gun whose business card read "Have Gun, Will Travel." Paladin did not fit the typical hired gun role. He was a tough, fast-shooting, affluent *nice guy*, who helped people in distress, towns under siege, kids in trouble, helpless women, and injured puppies. Despite being the good guy, Paladin always wore black. Paladin was a hired gun with character and integrity, and was extremely well schooled on his targets. Though he was paid to take people out for justifiable reasons, if he thought he was being hired erroneously or discovered his employer was actually a bad guy with questionable objectives, Paladin would turn on him and assist those he was hired to take out. This, however, was a 1950s television show where good and bad were made to be easily discernable.

Today's corporate hired guns bear no resemblance to Paladin. It is purely economic with them, and their own livelihood is dependent on their ability to execute both their mission and taking out the people who are their targets. They will accomplish their task with unflinching emotions and with expediency. The hired gun is highly visible and comes to the company with the sole objective of removing people. They never lurk in the shadows but rather make their presence and their mission known. They never identify their target in advance, and they never look to level the playing field. Everyone in the company knows why they're there; they just don't know who or how many have been targeted. The hired gun always believes their mission is "just"; after all, the company makes it no secret that it's hiring this individual, and as with James Bond, it has given this person a license to kill.

The hired gun can be the interim CEO, CFO, or some other C-level individual. This person can be the outside consultant brought in to look at the entire company or just a department. An interim department head, best practices consultant, and other similar names are all titles and positions the hired gun might carry. When hired guns arrive on the scene, many of the staff has no knowledge of who they are, and just like in the Clint Eastwood movie *Pale Rider*, people walk around asking, "Who is that guy anyway?" Hired guns are not always hired by the executives of the company. Many a board of directors has surprised CEOs with comments like: "Bill, the board feels we need to look at some of the operating procedures in the company, and we've decided to bring in a consultant, Mr. Hans Lugar. This has nothing to do with your performance; the board simply wants Mr. Lugar to provide an opinion and recommendation on company ops. We trust you'll cooperate with him fully." Now, if you're stupid enough to believe that, you shouldn't be the CEO.

We should be clear, though: the hired gun may not always be a "bad guy," but she will always be lethal to those who fall into her cross hairs. In some situations, the hired gun enters a "town gone bad"—or in modern terms, a highly distressed company. In many instances, some who get taken out deserve to be taken out. They have mismanaged, hoarded power, not provided for the corporate good, or been involved in a host of other failures. If in leadership, this person cannot dodge his participation in the failures that have arisen in the company. As a result, removal is the only option. Very often the sheriff sometimes has a group of deputies, some who have been accomplices and others who took the job thinking they can make the place better. In almost every instance, the individual at the top is dead, as are her closest associates. The chances of her dodging a bullet is unlikely because she was already dead, she just didn't know it. Some of the leadership's associates, however, particularly those with good intentions and positive actions, may find a way to dodge a bullet. They may even be able to become one of the hired gun's team. Are they selling out? It really depends on the situation.

Let's take the case of Vijay Mehta. Mr. Mehta had worked for Patientcare Pharmaceutical Incorporated for almost twenty-five years. He had joined after receiving his PhD in chemistry from a midsized southern college. He took on a midlevel research position within Patientcare's development organization, where his talent for innovation moved him up the company ranks rapidly. Now at fifty, he was very comfortable in his position as executive vice president of research and development for Patientcare's Specialty Pharmaceutical Group. With corporate sales of around $500 million per annum, the Specialty Products Group represented between 65 percent of Patientcare's overall sales. As a pharmaceutical company, Patientcare was always dependent on its specialty pharmaceutical line to drive bottom-line profits. Unfortunately, in the past three years Patientcare had taken a pretty good hit in profits because of its failure to develop new products and incrementally enhance existing products. For all leadership's intents, nothing had come out of the group's development organization for a considerable period of time.

The reality was, when Vijay was challenged regarding his group's performance, his responses were borderline arrogant, during which in fits of rage he would often cite his historical performance with the company or in some way deflect blame to some other individual or department, with the sales organization normally being his biggest target. Patientcare's CEO Gunter Shute and the board had always respected Vijay's capabilities and saw that he was compensated well for his early product development work and the patents he secured. Despite the CEO's efforts to impress upon Vijay that things in his organization needed to improve and that he might bring in an outside adviser to help Vijay and his team, Vijay privately dismissed Shute's comments as whining and his own worries that the board might oust him.

Vijay's reaction was immediate the morning he came into work to find MaryAnn Magnum sitting in his office. MaryAnn was a fifty-something executive with her own firm Magnum Consulting LLC. She was a no-nonsense professional with a PhD in chemical engineering from Stanford and a degree in pharmacy from the University of Rhode Island. She had founded two separate pharmaceutical companies, which she later took public and sold. Her many patents had made her a highly regarded individual in the pharmaceutical industry. Vijay knew immediately who she was, and though he inwardly wanted to storm down to Gunter's office and say, "What the hell is going on," he greeted MaryAnn cordially. That may have been the last cordial moment they shared. For the next two weeks, MaryAnn essentially became the Specialty Pharmaceutical Group's proctologist, and she wasn't using anesthesia. For Vijay, dodging bullets had already become an impossibility. MaryAnn would not buy into the deflections and the "blame game," and Vijay was rapidly running out of excuses with no cover in sight. In his attempts to appeal to the CEO, he was greeted with: "We'll have plenty of time to talk after MaryAnn completes her assessment."

About two more weeks passed upon the completion of the assessment, and there was very little feedback, let alone communications between the CEO and Vijay. Although Vijay made several attempts to garner information from both the CEO and CFO, he was fundamentally brushed off with comments like, "We will give you a complete group assessment once we've evaluated all the data provided." Vijay would attempt to thwart his concerns by telling himself that they were assessing the entire group and not just his leadership—an effort he himself didn't believe. On a Friday afternoon, three weeks from the completion of the group assessment, Vijay was asked by Shute's admin to come down to the CEO's office. Preparing himself for one final pitch to the CEO, Vijay walked with determination on his face and quickness in his step, but in his heart he knew he was a dead man walking.

MaryAnn had worked with precision and expediency, and there was never any doubt about the outcome. The synopsis Vijay was given relative to MaryAnn's report was pretty much a blur to him as he sat there along with the CFO and VP of human resources. He vaguely remembers something about "We thank you for your service to the company" and something else about "There comes a time for all executives to move on" and "We're sure you'll bring a great deal of value to whatever position you take in the future." That's about how he recalled it all as he was sitting on the freeway headed home. He had just finished hearing his own eulogy. On the following Monday, because of some help from MaryAnn, Vijay's replacement would be stepping into Vijay's former role. As for MaryAnn Magnum, she would be finishing up her assignment at another company. *"Have gun, will travel."*

One thing all hired guns know is that from the day they sign on as a hired gun, they also become a target. The difference is that most hired guns are consultants, like MaryAnn Magnum in our story, and so they're used to having guns aimed in their direction. They typically don't find a warm reception in the organizations they are hired by, and sometimes the very thing they are hired to do becomes an affront to those who hired them. You see, hired guns not only terrify the people they are hired to shoot but they terrify the people who hired them. In the aforementioned story, the CEO and his board had set their sights on Vijay, but there is nothing to say that the board couldn't have turned around and had MaryAnn take out the CEO. The ability of a hired gun to execute a plan is not only his biggest asset, it is his biggest liability, and this is why he rarely moves into executive roles at the companies who have retained him. Right or wrong, good or bad, the one thing all hired guns know is they must ride into the sunset when their job is complete. The new people they bring into power will always worry that that the hired gun has a few more bullets left in his pistol. Those who employed the hired gun will always be terrified by the fact that they gave this person too much power.

Some hired guns make the cardinal sin of accepting a position with those who hired them as a consultant. The result of this is either one of two outcomes. The first outcome is that of staying too long. When a hired gun ends up in this capacity, her own ability to execute blinds her to her own vulnerability. The assumed professional immortality she had in her consulting career carries over to her corporate career. She make the assumption that she know how to manage impeccably while those around her, with the exception of a few sycophants, are total incompetents. The power she assumes makes her believe that she has become invulnerable. Without realizing it, these individuals open themselves up to eventually being taken out by one of the other shooters discussed in this book. In such an instance, they will probably not know they're a target until they've been hit, because like Vijay, they are filled with hubris.

The second outcome of the consultant accepting a long-term position is that both he and the company's management come to realize that a great consultant is not always a great employee. If the consultant was truly astute, he would have never taken the position to begin with; if he is somewhat astute, he realizes his error and quickly goes back to consulting. If the CEO is more astute, he eliminates the problem himself (after all, he is the town marshal) and sends the consultant off to Boot Hill. So if you ever find yourself being a hired gun and choose to stick around, it is more than likely that someone may show up in town one day who can outdraw you.

CHAPTER 3

THE SNIPER: ANOTHER ONE BITES THE DUST

> *The Sniper must not be susceptible to emotions such as anxiety and remorse...*
> —CRAIG ROBERTS, CROSSHAIRS ON THE KILL ZONE: AMERICAN COMBAT SNIPERS, VIETNAM THROUGH OPERATION IRAQI FREEDOM

Ever get that sense in your company that people were being taken out right and left, and nobody seemed to know who was doing it or why they were doing it? Ever come into your office only to see a colleague packing up her things or perhaps just finding out the guy or gal who use to sit next to you was gone? Ever get the sense that people were dropping like flies but you just couldn't tell where the bullets were coming from? If you believe in the *Invasion of the Body Snatchers*, you've picked up the wrong book to read and should go get a bowl of ice cream and a Pepsi and flip on the Syfy channel. If you believe it's coming from the human resources organization, you should stop reading this book and go home, as you are already part of the walking dead. Wake up! Look around. This is real, and it's happening all around you.

On the corporate battleground, human resources represents either the obstetrician bringing a new life to be part of the company or the undertaker who is cleaning up after those who are already dead. If you're an existing employee at a company and the HR people are heading your way (and you're not about to celebrate your twenty-fifth year with the company), more than likely you've already been identified as a target and you're already lying in the mortuary.

Human resources is not the sniper. In point of fact, HR rarely knows who the sniper is; they are simply there to clean up after his mess and remove the evidence that there ever was a sniper.

In companies, there are no high steeples, rocky terrain, or tall walls for snipers to hide behind and locate their mark. There are no concrete walls or dark basements from which to take aim on their targets. Corporate snipers are invisible in plain sight; they are patient, and they are accurate. They are not "assassins," nor are they "hired guns," and they are much more than a cliché. In the majority of instances, they are colleagues, but not necessarily those with whom you have day-to-day interaction. In many cases, employees have a general knowledge of, or a relationship with, a company sniper; they just don't recognize the duality of what that person does. The sniper more than likely knows just about everything that is going on inside the company and has casual relationships with many of its employees. The sniper's targets are never random.

Snipers are not "bad guys," and more than likely they are highly beneficial and highly productive when looking out for the corporation's interests—that is, unless you're on the receiving end of what they do. Good corporate snipers watch and wait. Their target is not always defined, but they are always on the lookout for a target. Unlike the assassin, they do not pretend to like their mark but rather look for traits and actions that cause someone to become a target. In battle, a true sniper looks for small signs that give away a target's location: the movement of a bird suddenly flying away, a ripple in a puddle that had been still for some length of time, the sound of a pebble rolling down a mound, or a shift in the wind that carries a different smell. All these clues cause snipers to lock in on a given area. A brief reflection of the sun's light, a fraction of a piece of cloth behind a wall, or a wisp of hair hanging outside a pillar unexpectedly...all can identify a potential target. The sniper does not rush to take a shot but rather sits and waits.

Have you ever worked with an individual who is always worried about his or her job? Who hasn't seen one of these "nervous Nellies" in a company? These are the ones who avoid risk at all costs. They are always looking to cover their ass and assign blame. When an announcement is made within the company, they are always second-guessing what the real meaning is. They constantly look for conspiracies and subtle or not so subtle changes in the company or operating procedure that are suspicious to them. They are also the company's storytellers and rumormongers, and they never realize that the outcome of their actions is to make themselves a target. These kinds of people inadvertently draw attention to themselves in their effort to avoid becoming anyone's target. For a sniper on a mission, these are the first ones the sniper takes out when a company is going through a transition.

The most obvious fact in the corporate world is that companies are always in transition. Business goes up, and business goes down. The company is going to buy another company or going to be sold to another company. It's going lean or adding fat. It doesn't really matter—change is ever present, and some things are simply going to be different. Because of this ever-occurring process, snipers are always in demand and always ready to be deployed. When I ran companies, I had what I called the 25 percent rule. Simply, this rule asks the questions: "What do we do if we lose 25 percent of our business tomorrow?" and "What do we do if we expand our business by 25 percent tomorrow?" In both instances, there was always a plan, and that plan always included a head-count change whether the business was expanding or contracting. Change always meant personnel changes, and personnel changes meant always having a list of those who would no longer be with the company. Typically, that list was shared with those to be engaged as corporate snipers. Usually they had the input early on as to who the most obvious targets were and the order in which they were to be taken out.

When businesses are sold, merged, or in a turnaround phase, snipers become very active. Fundamentally, they lay in wait a psychological mile away from the bus depot and they watch, keeping leadership informed about what they see. The people at the bus station don't see the sniper. When the bus finally pulls up, a group of people anxiously jump on the bus, ready to head for their new destination. These people are safe…for now. Another group stands on the station platform and never moves forward. Even a warning shot will not move these people, and so the sniper(s) doesn't waste a bullet. He has his first targets. All these targets are easy because they were never prepared for the war and failed to see the signals around them. They thought of their nonaction as action, never realizing it meant their demise. They didn't have a prayer when it came to dodging a bullet.

Once the sniper is finished with these people, he spots a group with one foot on the bus and one foot off the bus. They go through repeated gyrations and emotional debate. The sniper fires a warning shot, wounding one of them. In a heartbeat, a small group immediately jumps to perceived safety on the bus (nobody there has been shot yet). Another group turns away from the bus and immediately heads for the depot. They don't make it. Part of the remaining group has their foot on the bus while a small portion stands behind the bus peeking out to see who's shooting at them. They don't make it either. The bus finally pulls away, and it is the point of reckoning for the remainder of the people. If they don't jump aboard, their fate is guaranteed. If they do at this point, their fate is left in question.

Ever seen any of these scenarios play out? Were you on the bus? Off the bus? In between? The sniper? Or the person sending orders to the sniper? Or do you even know? What did you learn? If you work in a highly volatile business, you should be prepared. If you work for a large stable corporation, expect the unexpected. If you work for the government, administrations always change so change is forthcoming. And if you work in a Main Street American small business, know that you will always be vulnerable.

It should be noted that though most snipers rise from within a business, business are not immune from external snipers. Government agencies, for example, are notorious for using professional snipers to take down a corporate executive or business. For highly public figures and companies, the media has its own version of snipers who want nothing more than to take out some individual or company. Can you think of companies and organizations that have fallen under IRS scrutiny or corporate leaders who have been taken out, never knowing who really fired the shot? Whatever the case, the sniper almost always walks away unscathed—unless, of course, there is another sniper with her sights set on him.

CHAPTER 4

FRIENDLY FIRE: "AIN'T SO FRIENDLY"

Isn't it amazing how much friendly fire
resembles friendly stupidity?
—*HARRY ROZAKIS*

There is no greater disappointment in the corporate world (and in life) than to take a bullet as a result of "friendly fire." Friendly fire can happen virtually at any time, even when there is no good reason for anyone or anything to take a shot at you. Although it is more likely to take place during a corporate upheaval, it can just as easily occur when the world seems to be running smoothly. It can happen to those who have complete career satisfaction, to those totally disgruntled with their employer or co-workers, and even to those who are totally apathetic toward their corporate position. In some instances, it results from an off-the-cuff comment made during a social conversation. On other occasions, a person may be simply providing advice on how to improve the company or enhance a coworker's job performance. These comments are shared inadvertently but interpreted in a completely wrong way, which results in unintended consequences. This is information being shared among friends that not-so-friendly people use to their advantage.

The difficulty with friendly fire is that it is never expected and, as the name suggests, comes from someone who is supposed to be looking out for us. It doesn't happens because someone close to us takes aim at us. Rather, they believe something you did or said caused someone to take a shot at you, and in response, they are trying to save you from yourself.

On other occasions, friendly fire occurs because one of your friends or supporters believes she's taking action to help you advance your career. I remember a story I heard about an individual who was brought into a company by the existing CEO (let's call him Joe Coltrain) as his heir apparent. The individual had fostered a great relationship with Joe and was brought in at a senior level to prepare to take over the CEO job when Joe stepped down in six months. Many in the company were led to believe that the new employee was to be the next CEO, and so they aligned themselves with this individual The heir's friendship with Joe was strong, and he believed the positive feedback he was receiving from Joe was based on his performance. He also believed that the message regarding his performance was being taken to the board of directors. After Joe went to the board to pass on the accolades of his hand-chosen successor, the board responded by telling Joe that he was on his way out the door and that a new CEO had already been hired. Can you imagine the impact on the heir apparent who left his prior company specifically for a perceived better opportunity, only to find out his friend had no power or authority to advance the heir? Imagine the vulnerability of all the people who had befriended the heir thinking he would be their new boss. Would they soon fall victim to friendly fire.

Friendly fire also occurs because an individual close to us doesn't recognize the bad guys from the good guys. Acting in a way he believes will benefit you, he unwittingly passes on information or comments you've shared, thinking he can advance your position by sharing them with people he believes are "good guys" and who also have your best interest in mind. He tells a colleague or someone senior to you about your expressed interest in a new position that has opened up. What he doesn't know is the person he is sharing this with is lobbying with management for the same position or has been grooming someone else in the company for that position. Unbeknown to you, you are now in the cross hairs of someone you don't know or someone you would never perceive as a shooter.

How many times have you heard of individuals who are good employees but espouse ideas that are not consistent with how the company is managed? The individual may have a great idea on how the company can perform better but is smart enough to know it is inconsistent with management's thinking and chooses not to share until she believes it's an appropriate time. Unfortunately, that individual makes the error of sharing that idea with a friend, who tells someone, who tells someone. Management, through the grapevine, picks up these comments and now perceives they come from someone who would undermine them. Once again, the efforts of a friend or colleague have put a target on this individual.

I know of women who are moving up the corporate ladder and are true contributors to their organization. They learn they are pregnant but also realize they have a few months before the baby will be "showing" and recognize they can accomplish a lot in the months before they need to go on maternity leave. Anxious to share the good news, they approach their best friend at work and share, in confidence, the great news. Of course, the good friend, in confidence, begins sharing the good news with others, and finally it makes its way to management. You can imagine the chagrin of the woman when she learns there's a great new project team that she won't be assigned to since, given that she will be departing on maternity leave, the boss, with his newly found information, has decided to look out for the health and well-being of the woman, and directed her toward a task that will be "more timely and less stressful." What a great guy!

All these good friends, sometimes even the boss, are "looking out for your best interest," but the target they've painted on you couldn't be bigger. Taking a bullet doesn't always mean you've been terminated from your position, but it can very well mean you've had an opportunity shot out from under you.

The person who hits you with friendly fire is not to be confused with the "the one who walks in the shadows of plain sight" discussed in the next chapter. Friendly fire comes from those who truly believe in you. Their desire to help is sometimes so great that they don't realize the ramifications of what they're doing. When you are finally killed or wounded, those responsible for friendly fire ask themselves questions like: "Well, how could this have happened? I didn't know he was on so-and-so's shit list, did you? How did so-and-so know she even wanted that position? How could the boss have possibly found out you were pregnant?" Quite obviously, there is no accountability by "your friend," but by God he's going to ferret out the culprit who got you screwed. Then there are the ones who sit there saying, "I just don't know how this happened."

CHAPTER 5

THE ASSASSIN: "WALKING IN THE SHADOWS OF PLAIN SIGHT!"

> *I think in the corridors of power these dangerous*
> *kinds of orders are issued in a much more*
> *vague way, passed down two or three levels of*
> *command before they're given to the assassin.*
> —EDDIE CAMPBELL, SCOTTISH ARTIST

In the world of dodging bullets and shooting back, there is no worse character, and no better tool, than "the one who walks in the shadows of plain sight," or the assassin. This is the stealthy individual who appears unarmed, gets real close, and then uses the most powerful weapons in her arsenals: i.e., words, deceit, lies, and suspicions. Yes, the assassin will shoot you in the back and you'll never see it coming. Unlike friendly fire, where there is no intent to do harm, these lethal technicians set their plan and establish a relationship, and when the time is right, they blindside their victim. Assassins are pragmatic in their quest for elimination because they are indifferent to the benefits that may be derived for those who hire them. The transactions itself is all about the remuneration they receive for their efforts.

The motives and the objectives of the assassins' employer can vary, but *their* objectives are always self-serving. Perhaps you're in the way of a promotion or a raise. In other cases, they serve no one but themselves, and their actions may be specific to a known or unknown personal link to what's going on inside the company. It could be that you already beat them out for a position they wanted but you were totally unaware they were shooting for the same position. In some cases, it can be a pure power play designed to put someone they are closely linked to into power (or perhaps even themselves). Whether it is cash, a promotion, a position, or a forthcoming opportunity, the assassin is in some way a beneficiary.

The assassins are the worst of all "shooters" because they pretend to be your friend. They may go out with you, play sports with you, and share what appear to be secrets with you, all in the quest to get closer to you. They may go as far as getting together with families so your spouses can become friendly. An assassin's villainy—though it can be driven by anger, revenge, enrichment, and other similar factors—most often in the corporate world is truly an instrument of someone else whose motivations are identical to those attributed to the assassin. Although they most often operate solo, unless it is personal, the assassin always receives their instructions from someone else. The assassin may not really know who is behind the assignment, but his charter is not to understand but simply to execute.

Assassins and those who hire them have to be regarded as opportunists. They can come forth at an individual level, but they also appear in groups at the corporate level in the instances of hostile takeovers. They are pragmatists, and if a situation arises where taking action on their part represents gain or satisfaction (whether perceived or real), they act. At a corporate level, it could involve a partner, a competitor, a customer, or just some external group that wants to jump on what they see as a low-cost-of-entry business opportunity. It is the target's vulnerability that prompts them to take action, and so they relentlessly pursue the ultimate demise of that target. Assassins are very good at justifying that those they shoot from behind were probably going to get it anyway so why not help them. They may convince themselves that taking out an individual or an entire company is an act of inevitability for a multitude of reasons. This self-deceit may make them feel righteous about their actions, despite the ramifications to the target individual or company. Assassins, whether justifiably engaged or maliciously motivated, are results-oriented, and those results will often have a major impact on those they've taken out.

Assassins are not "hired guns." They come from inside the company and outside the company. When not motivated for their own selfish gain, they follow orders from the top and, in point of fact, can be two or three levels down within the hierarchy of the corporation. A friend, a colleague, a supplier, and even a customer can all be assassins. They are always on a singular mission, and that mission is to take down a business or an individual. Although assassins can engage targets directly, they can also act surreptitiously to set up a situation that will have a disastrous outcome for those they have targeted. The truly proficient assassin on occasion will get you to unwittingly help him construct and plan your own demise.

A second-tier high-tech company, Pequod Technologies Inc., had for several years been losing business and had seen its share price plummet. The board had repeatedly brought in weak leadership, mostly due to its own internal divisiveness. After an intense search by a first-rate recruitment firm, they found a new CEO, Dick Remington. Unlike a hired gun, Dick played out the role of being the new sheriff in town. His charter was to fundamentally turn Pequod around. Unlike his predecessors, Dick was a no-nonsense, nonpolitical executive who laid out strategies and saw that they were executed. In the process of making substantive changes, Dick removed people from the company who were not prepared to make the changes he was implementing. In some cases, he removed long-time executives, some who had been politically friendly with specific board members. A key move that Dick made was to bring in a new CFO, Andrew Flintlock. Dick and Andrew became quick allies.

Under Dick's leadership, Pequod began a focused and substantive turnaround. Over the next few years, the stock price rose dramatically, revenue and profits improved, and its market share was expanding. Externally, the business was looking good, but internally it had faced a significant number of challenges. The divisiveness within Pequod's board had been ongoing, and with a divided board, Dick's decisions, despite the positive results, would routinely alienate different factions within the board. Up until this point, Andrew and Dick were able to ward off the board's objections and petty arguments. Although a strong ally, Andrew also wanted more, so Dick laid out a path for him to become the chief operating officer.

Pequod was approaching a strategic inflection point that could permanently and substantially determine the company's success or failure. For Dick, the direction was obvious, but he knew the loudest and sometimes most influential members of the board were against his strategy. Dick also knew that as long as he and Andrew held firm in their position, they would be able to take Pequod to greater success. At the next board meeting, Dick presented his strategy. As he did, he could see that the board was significantly more political and hostile than on prior occasions. Despite an extremely credible argument,

Dick was repeatedly blocked. You can imagine his astonishment and despair when the board chair stated that members of the board had been working with Andrew on an alternate strategy that was more to their liking financially and that they would be replacing Dick with Andrew as CEO. *"Et tu, Brute?"* Dick knew immediately this was not only a deathblow to himself, but it would be a deathblow to the entire company. He was right. But like Troy's Cassandra, you may be able to predict the future, but it doesn't mean anyone will believe you.

The Pequod scenario has been played out in business and in politics for generations. Some have seen it coming, some have dodged the bullet, and some have fired back unmercifully. In some instances, the assassin's strike was a necessary but beneficial evil, while in other instances it has brought down kings and empires.

> *Uneasy lies the head that wears a crown*
> —*WILLIAM SHAKESPEARE,* HENRY THE IV

It can happen at the highest corporate and political levels or within a specific department or agency. As the Shakespeare quote implies, even those in charge should never let themselves get too comfortable. Even kings must see the gun before it is in the shooter's hand. Assassins eliminate tyrants, and they eliminate the good and the great. Assassins are not born, they are made, and their reward takes all kinds of forms. Can you see an assassin coming at you? No, so "trust no one."

> *War is the statesman's game, the priest's delight,*
> *the lawyer's jest, the hired assassin's trade.*
> —*PERCY BYSSHE SHELLEY*

CHAPTER 6

THE GUNSLINGER: WYATT EARP

> *I think we need a gunslinger*
> *Somebody tough to tame this town*
> *Think we need a gunslinger*
> *There'll be justice all around*
> —JOHN FOGERTY, LYRICS FROM "GUNSLINGER"

Gunslingers are typically those individuals seeking to make a name for themselves. In the workplace, gunslingers can be homegrown or a new recruit of the business. In either instance, they are the type of individual who is attempting to move quickly through the ranks of a department or a company. They are dangerous because they always shoot first and ask questions later. They're the Wyatt Earps of the business, and though they're capable of cleaning up Tombstone, they leave a lot of bodies behind. Like many shooters, gunslingers are rarely random in their selection of who to shoot. Unlike a sniper or an assassin, a gunslinger can be extremely overt about how and who they want to shoot. They know who their targets are and how they will benefit from the shooting.

It not uncommon in the earlier stages of a gunslinger's career with a company or business unit to see them taking shots at soft and easy targets without any real logic or reason. Their object is to get the attention of others, both those who would fear them and those who would make use of them. The stature of a target is of no concern to the gunslinger unless he or she believes that the target is, at least in the near term, better armed than they are.

Individually, the gunslinger has been with the company long enough to believe he has knowledge of the "lay of the land" and can make a few early kills to begin to establish his reputation as "someone to be reckoned with." That reputation is reinforced early by his superiors, whose acceptance of the gunslinger's actions is also demonstrated through some rapid promotions and associated pay increases. Early on, he can be viewed as a results-oriented hard charger and a real potential contributor to the company. The few bodies he's left in the dust are viewed as justifiable kills that probably weren't going to make it anyway. Peers can quickly become sycophants, and his subordinates are often timid and afraid. Wise executives see this shooter as a necessary evil but in many instances realize that this same necessary evil could easily aspire to moving to the top of the food chain. Gunslingers may have them in their sites, and so they always keep their powder dry, just in case.

Although they can be extremely overt when it comes to entering into a gunfight, gunslingers do differ in terms of style. There are those who are out-spoken, often conceited, in your face, and challenging. Others let their actions speak for them but never cover up or mislead about where their intentions lie. The gunslinger's position in the company can be almost anything, from a new sales guy or lab tech, to the CEO of the company. The CEOs are usually those who ascended to their position by being gunslingers and continue in that role to ensure they can pick off any challengers to their position. Sometimes their field of battle is limited to the department or unit within which they operate, while other times their aspirations are at the corporate level.

Boards have been known to hire gunslingers but not in the same capacity that they bring in a hired gun. When a board brings in a gunslinger, the intent may be to drive a turnaround in a poorly performing business or to focus on the expansion of the company (as with an external transaction such as an M&A deal). Gunslingers on the corporate battlefield are particularly adept when it comes to aggressive or hostile takeovers. They are smart, cunning, and effective, which in the case of many companies is exactly what they need. In industry, there are many legendary gunslingers known to have left a trail of bodies behind them, but through their ability to execute they have achieved phenomenal results, which have led to long-term benefits and profitability for their businesses. Lou Gerstner of American Express and IBM fame comes to mind, along with Larry Bossidy of AlliedSignal and Honeywell. Some gun-slingers may never become the CEO, but when there is a "mess" to clean up, the gunslinger perhaps can be the most effective of all shooters.

CHAPTER 7

STRAY BULLETS

Doesn't matter how good your bullets
are if you don't aim carefully.
—BRANDON SANDERSON, THE ALLOY OF LAW

When I did the original preparation for this book, I didn't have this section in mind. There could have been an argument made for including this part in the "collateral damage" section. As I gave it further thought, however, I came to realize that this book would be incomplete without this section. Now, oddly enough, my motivation resulted from the area in which I live in North Carolina. Having lived most of my adult life in California and as an expatriate around the world, hearing gunfire on a day-to-day basis is something to which I have never been accustomed. (I have dodged a few bullets in other parts of the world, but coups in Thailand, protests in South Africa, mobs in London, and riots in the Philippines are best left for another book.)

One evening when my wife and I were out for a walk, we could hear the sounds of gunfire in the woods, not all that far away from our home. "Did you ever wonder where the bullets go when they miss?" I asked both quizzically and naively. "I mean, really, if they don't hit something, do they just keep traveling until finally dropping to the ground?" My wife replied that she hadn't given it much thought and gave me a somewhat odd look, but then she got the gist of what I was asking. Now, I don't have an issue with gun ownership, and I certainly don't mind people using them for recreation and sport, but I really don't know where all those stray bullets go. I've never found one just lying on the ground when I've been hiking through the forest or up in the mountains. Have you ever found a slug just lying on the ground? I do know that people miss more of their targets than they hit. So where do all those stray bullets go? All of this got me to immediately start thinking about bullets fired in business that go astray.

My experience has taught me that in a professional environment stray bullets don't stop till they hit someone. Just because someone has a target on their back or because a shooter is an excellent shot, it doesn't mean the target is always hit the first time. Unlike my previous example of missed targets in North Carolina, missed targets in the corporate world often mean that someone else has been hit. There are also instances where targets have been hit and the bullet goes straight through the target and picks someone else off as well. Even a shooter who is typically accurate will have little regard for someone else who gets hit during the effort to bring down her primary target.

Let's consider how something like this occurs. A vice president of sales at Bartholomew & Company, John Ableman, and his team have been under fire during a tough economic market. Their biggest account is unhappy, and this news reaches John's boss, Executive VP Ed Glock. Some members of the sales team supporting him are also highly unhappy about how things have been going, but it's difficult to say whether it's because of poor management, a weak market, or simply because John leans on them for a higher level of performance and better results. Whatever the case, these are unsettling times at Bartholomew, and Glock feels he needs to take action and make a change, with John being his primary target. This is not to say that the John and his sales team are necessarily poor performers but rather that a perception has been created by the customer and others within the company, making this perception the new reality.

Between John and his sales team is John's director of sales, Ben Goodman. Ben has been with the company for fifteen years. He has seen the company through its highs and lows, and has always been a steady performer. Ben has weathered many business and political storms in his years at Bartholomew, and it would seem he's about to face another. He has a good relationship with John, and philosophically and operationally they are on the same page. Ben has been the intermediary between the sales team and John, but given his loyalty to the company and to John, he is going to execute plans and actions as they are presented to him.

Ed Glock feels compelled to take action, and he is prepared to set his sights on John Ableman. Glock advises the CEO of his planned action. During their conversation, Glock who is prepared to move quickly, is reminded by the CEO that he (the CEO) was the one who recruited John from a supplier because he was so impressed by his performance. Nevertheless, the CEO agrees some action needs to be taken. After a lengthy discussion, Glock is instructed to put John on notice that things need to change. He then tells John to terminate both Ben Goodman and the salesman who deals with the account that launched the complaint.

John follows his orders, and without hesitation he terminates Goodman and the account salesperson. The stray bullets that hit Goodman and the sales rep are a total blindside. A bullet meant for their boss buzzed right past him and headed directly for them. One moment they were sitting at their desks, and the next moment they were being walked out of the building. It could be argued that they had no reaction time to dodge the bullets that hit them. Or did they? Were they paying attention? Was there evidence to suggest that something was going to happen? The answer is, they probably weren't paying attention, and as a result they ignored the evidence around them. Was this a bullet they could have dodged? Maybe not, but they could have prepared for the possibility. If there is a moral to this story, it's that a good man sometimes gets hit by stray bullets and an able man knows how to dodge them.

CHAPTER 8

THE POSSE: "MOB RULE"

> *Butch Cassidy: How many are following us?*
> *Sundance Kid: All of 'em.*
> *Butch Cassidy: All of 'em? What's*
> *the matter with those guys?*

*P*osse might as well be another word for a mob (no, not organized crime) of so-called "do-gooders" who claim to have justice on their side but act very often with reckless abandon. Even when their cause is fundamentally just, their methods may not be. The mob mentality has a uniqueness of its own. When it begins, it is pervasive, and if you are on the receiving end of its wrath, things are not going to turn out well for you. Whether in business or politics, when a posse is formed its members are rarely objective and more than often extremely emotional. In the Old West, a posse was formed when it was perceived someone had committed some kind of crime and was running or hiding in order to avoid justice. Posses and mobs are rarely interested in real justice and most often are not interested in the truth. In many cases, they have already made up their minds, and their intention is only to take out the perceived wrongdoer(s). This makes for a "shoot first, ask questions later" mentality and never works out well for those being pursued.

The mob is always dangerous because it can be formed very quickly, and the assumed premise under which it is formed does not always offer clarity of purpose. In other instances, the motivation behind the mob's formation may be clear, but unfortunately that premise is either wrong or misunderstood. Those who join a posse are usually not vetted by anyone, including the organizers of that posse. Sometimes posses are made up of voyeurs and thrill seekers, as well as those who have a specific mission in mind. The posse is always better armed and more dangerous than the alleged law breaker. Some individuals, in point of fact, have broken the rules and punishing them is necessary, but the punishment, though it should fit the crime, usually doesn't when it is the posse that becomes judge, jury, and executioner. In other instances, individuals (sometimes groups) are singled out by the posse for nothing more than the inference of wrongdoing. Then there are those individuals who truly want to take out an individual but use the cover of a posse or mob to accomplish this end. Haven't we all seen the instance where someone's opposition or competition "throws shit against the wall to see if it sticks"? Unfortunately, this occurs more often in business and politics than we would like to admit. When it happens, the individual with nefarious objectives organizes a mob to cover up the fact that he is the actual shooter.

In the Old West movies, posses came from one of two places. They were generated in the town where the alleged act was committed, or they came from a group outside of the town *a la Butch Cassidy and the Sundance Kid*. In either case, posses were both purposeful and lethal. Business, like politics, routinely sees the emergence of mobs and the mob mentality, and that mob can be either internal to the company or external from the company. There are typically some very distinct differences between an internally generated mob and an externally driven mob. Let's take a look at each of these.

Much to our chagrin, society continues to exhibit more and more political correctness, and the "speech police" are ready to jump on anyone who says something of which they don't approve. In doing so, these people now also become the "thought police" because they attempt to attribute a motivation behind someone's speech, which may not even be in accord with the person's intentions. It's amazing how quickly some are ready to throw out the First Amendment when those who disagree with them speak. Dodging bullets fired by an external posse is the most challenging because the bullets can come from so many different directions. There was a time when honesty was the best policy, but today an executive runs the risk of having his career and even his company ruined by something he says publicly or is overheard saying privately. We are not talking here about those using disparaging language to vilify an individual or group, and we're not speaking to those who would initiate unjust actions against an individual or a group. What we are addressing are those expressing an opinion or their position on a corporate, political, or social issue.

We would all agree that a posse may absolutely be necessary to go after those who commit heinous acts or are engaged in reprehensible corporate behavior. In this instance, Enron and Bernie Madoff come to mind. Though applicable to these two villains, the challenge is: where does the line get drawn on what's heinous and reprehensible and what isn't when the issue is more subjective? If a company or its leadership has knowingly been polluting drinking water, or dispersing hazardous waste, or some other despicable act, then taking group action makes sense. No one would argue that a character like Bernie Madoff deserved what he got and possibly much more. This, however, is not what's being alluded to at this juncture. There are many businesspeople who are honest and fair-minded, and believe they are acting in the interest of their people, the community, and their business, only to find that a small group opposes them vehemently and will go to great lengths to bring them down.

We still live in a free-market economy, and every individual has the right to do business with whomever they choose as long as it is constitutional and legally acceptable. People always discriminate on how they buy. Individuals routinely make decisions on what restaurants or stores they frequent based on product value and quality, customer service, and overall costs. The messages people send can be a strong signal to the management of a company as to whether they offer a good product, good service, or an agreeable price. These are forces that drive changes in the market, allowing strong companies to survive and weaker companies to fade away. Unfortunately, there are posses out there that would like to inflict punitive action against those who think differently than they do. In days past, large corporations could be impacted by the print and written media outlets. Small business was relatively isolated except for the occasional unhappy customer or disgruntled employee. Today, with social media, no one is immune from criticism, which almost always goes unvetted. Even small businesses can be destroyed at a national level because a posse chooses to single them out.

Companies big and small are run by people and employ people. What a surprise! Human beings were never created to be perfect. They were never meant to think identically, and they rarely agree 100 percent with their leadership. Leadership comes in all forms, from all races and ethnic and religious backgrounds. In the United States, corporate leadership is not typically given, with a few exceptions, but rather earned. Yes, there are a handful of companies where nepotism and cronyism come into play or where preferences are exhibited, but the great thing about the United States and most capitalistic societies is that if you don't like the way a company is being managed, you can leave.

These days, we see a far angrier and more bitter approach toward those who manage and work in the private sector. There is an attitude that all executives and corporate leaders are evil, when the reality is, just like any segment of society, that there are those who are good and those who are bad (or more appropriately, incompetent). I've yet to find the perfect human being, but if I did, I can only imagine how uninteresting he or she would be. Most people forget that not everyone carrying a C-level title is making a fortune. Politicians will scream about C-level salaries, but no one says a word about the ballplayer who earns a hundred times what the hot-dog vendor earns, or the movie star who gets ten million dollars for one film, or the politician who earns two hundred and fifty thousand dollars per speech, while the boom operator or the political staffer makes a fraction of that amount. The reality is, most individuals running companies are "working stiffs." Their companies are small, they put in double-duty-hour weeks, and they create jobs for others whom they must pay before they pay themselves. They are simply the people who learned early that working hard brings a better return than not working hard. Yet there are posses in society that feel that if an executive or a management team takes an action contrary to what they believe, then they have the right to engage in far more malicious action against these leaders. They engage in considerably more than just not using their product or frequenting their stores; they seek to vilify them in the court of public opinion, very often being loose with the truth and applying their own interpretation to it. This is by no means unique to one side of the political and social spectrum. It happens on all sides, and in some cases, opposing sides unite against a third party if it suits their business and political interests. When you are attacked by a posse built on emotion and subjectivism, dodging bullets becomes a significant challenge.

When posses are internal to companies, they can be made up of leadership, boards of directors, organized labor, departmental staff, or any combination thereof. Forming these types of posses at times can prove to be very valuable to a company, while at other times it creates the dysfunctionality that can take a company to its knees. When necessary, an individual or group of whistleblowers may emerge within a company's labor force. Companies make mistakes, but it is how they address and correct their mistakes that will determine whether their management and the company itself will be taken down. The auto industry, the chemical industry, the pharmaceutical industry, and even government administrations have found themselves in this predicament. When they react swiftly and take corrective action, they can deflect or mitigate the impact of a posse, or redirect intelligence that will support the actions under scrutiny and offset them with facts. However, when management is "wishy-washy" in its response, or leadership starts scrambling to point fingers, this not only causes posses to get bigger and more impactful, but it creates more posses, which begin probing into everything, and rightfully so. How often have we heard of companies or individuals who failed to "get out in front" of an issue? Remember BP in the Gulf? Instead of falling on its sword and stepping up with immediate solutions, company executives demonstrated an outrageous level of hubris, which nearly destroyed them. Talk about putting a gun to your head. Companies should always realize that doing the right thing and going on the offensive is a way of shooting back without ever pulling the trigger.

Posses arise in small and big companies alike. Fortunately for small companies, unless there are problems that have national impact, posses don't get much notoriety—the one exception being if social media is used to blow a local situation out of proportion. Assuming there is no discrimination, violence, or other morally objectionable action taking place, the small company can typically stay out of the fray. Perhaps, in a worst-case scenario, local media picks up the story, or perhaps, depending on the area and the locality, some resident brings up the situation at a town hall meeting or public event. However, when a company is big enough to warrant national attention, then it has to deal with the biggest and most ruthless posse of all: the national media, followed these days by the social media mob. The more sensational the national media perceives a story to be, the greater the number of times it will appear and the longer the news cycle may run. The national media is not a single posse, however; it is many posses made up journalists, pundits, know-it-alls, and news people from television, print, web, and radio. As we have already indicated, there are companies that clearly bring the wrath of the posse upon themselves, but there are also instances where the media posse goes on a witch hunts in highly subjective ways predicated strictly on perception and unsubstantiated information. Negative stories, whether real or false, capture the attention of viewers, readers, and listeners.

In the case of companies that are the cause of their own downfall, the media may in fact be delivering an invaluable service. Again, one thinks of Enron, the Veterans Administration, BP, and others who have committed acts or made decisions that were highly damaging to others and the general public. In these situations, we have seen reputations destroyed, profits crumble, and in some instances individuals jailed or fined significantly, much to the satisfaction of the public and the victims. The hubris demonstrated by these executives is undeniable, and the lack of integrity unconscionable. Study these companies, and you will see throughout their history that many individuals have been taken out by an array of shooters only so these arrogant executives could keep their dirty little secrets hidden. The sad story for those employees who labored as good employees within those companies is that they ultimately become collateral damage or get hit by stray bullets. When posses act against these types of executives and companies, they serve an ideal purpose, and the intent is always to make right what has gone wrong. Sadly, the "making right" aspect can get lost, as the posse's focus is punishing the evil while forgetting about the good.

When posses are wrong and act impetuously, the impact on their targets is debilitating at best and catastrophic at worst. After individuals or organizations have been sliced and diced with a negative spin and false data, where do they go to regain their reputations and their lives? Negative stories always make the headlines, while retractions are placed on page seventeen or the end of a broadcast. On the Internet, you will be lucky to ever find a retraction. The posse dissipates, having done almost irrevocable damage, with little thought about what follows for the individual or institution once cleared of all wrongdoing. As we said, posses can do a great deal of positive things in bad situations, assuming the parameters for "bad" are clearly defined.

Before becoming part of a posse or leading a posse one needs to consider a number of things. What is the source of the evidence against the party or parties? How was the information uncovered and by who? Has all information and data been validated and reconfirmed by third parties? What is the anticipated outcome the posse hopes to achieve? Has the posse considered the impact on others, whether or not the posse's formation is right or wrong? Asking these types of questions can go a long way toward protecting innocent people and innocent companies while shutting down the guilty.

CHAPTER 9

GUNSMOKE

*I've seen a lot of men buried up here on Boot Hill,
and most of them really earned what they got. They
cheated at cards, robbed banks, stole horses, murdered
innocent men, and picked fights with friend and enemy
alike. They lived and died as though they'd never
heard of the law, and they treated me like a trespasser.
Someone who had no right to interfere with their
bloody little games. But I shot it out with 'em anyway,
and I guess I'll go right on doing it. As long as I last.*
—*JAMES ARNESS AS MATT DILLON*, GUNSMOKE

I loved the television show *Gunsmoke* when I was a little kid, but if you're under the age of fifty-five, you may not have a clue what I'm talking about. *Gunsmoke* was a television western starring James Arness, who played the marshal of Dodge City, Matt Dillion. Matt had a sidekick named Chester, a medical doctor friend named "Doc" (original), and a sweetheart who ran the local saloon named Miss Kitty. Dodge was a relatively peaceful town, but every now and then someone would try to muck things up and would have to square off with Marshal Dillon. As a kid, it was clear to me that none of these bad guys ever watched the show, because if they did they'd know that Marshal Dillon never loses. Unfortunately, there was at least one person a week who was going to have to answer to the marshal. A lot of the times, it was because these bad guys were out taking potshots at the good townspeople of Dodge. The great things about this show was, you always knew who the good guys and the bad guys were. As far as the show was concerned, Marshal Dillon always took out the bad guys, because being bad meant not following the law of the town. An interesting question is, what would happen if one of the perceived bad guys wasn't necessarily bad? The simple answer is: "Buddy, get out of Dodge."

Look at any company where the CEO or chairman has been around for a long time, and you may find a Marshal Matt Dillon, Will Kane, or Wyatt Earp. In today's world, one might look at John Chambers (Cisco), Larry Ellison (Oracle), Jamie Dimon (J. P. Morgan), Tom Watson(IBM) , and many others in all type of industries as being Matt Dillon types. In early American industry Vanderbilt, Rockefeller, Morgan, and Carnegie would have all fallen into this category. From the fictional Matt Dillon to all these captains of industry, they represented strong, steadfast individuals who exuded confidence and certainty through their actions. Fundamentally, they believed they were "right," and to challenge their authority and their positions meant you were wrong, whether you were or not. These greater-than-life characters exuded a perceived stability that few would be willing to disrupt. Like Marshal Dillon, backing down from a fight was not in the cards, particularly when you knew you would always win. Although there are many a business school that would argue that this is not how you manage in today's world, these leaders still exist and will continue to exist in the future. The only question is, what's to be done when they're wrong?

In this reality of dodging bullets and shooting back, the *Gunsmoke* scenario might be the easiest to deal with, or the most lethal. As we will discuss later in the book, dodging a bullet under this scenario may be among the easiest of challenges. Part of the reason for this is that the marshal isn't out looking for a fight; he's looking for order, and he gets to define what "order" is. Very often he doesn't even anticipate fights because he is confident no one would be willing to engage in a fight he knows he will lose. For the majority of individuals, working in a company with a marshal is easy. If you don't engage, if you keep the status quo, you'll never have to dodge a bullet.

The CEOs who are illustrative of the Matt Dillons of the world typically (but not always) run good companies. Few, however, as noted in Jim Collins's book *Good to Great*, run great companies. There are a tremendous number of good companies. We see and deal with them every day. Private, public, for-profit, not-for-profit, government agencies (yes, there are a few good ones), and big and small companies…they all do good things, make good products, and even make a profit. But few, if any, of these companies and organizations are great. Few will ever achieve *peak performance*. The executives of these companies know how to run good companies, but unfortunately many of them have no idea how to run a great company. So now comes the rub. What if there are people in these good companies who want to see their company become great? What if there is an individual(s) who believes that the introduction of new ideas, new products, and new concepts can drive that good company to a level of peak performance that makes them a great company? What happens when these people present these ideas to a single-minded Matt Dillon type and he shoots the ideas down?

This scenario plays out constantly in older established companies, but it also exists in the companies of Silicon Valley and other geographic areas of innovation, where change is constant. A Matt Dillon type doesn't have to be with the company for twenty-five years. He can just as easily be the founder who has only been around for three to five years or less. In either scenario, his organization recognizes his accomplishments and his leadership, but it also recognizes that when it comes to how the company operates, there are no forks in the road, only the chosen path. This doesn't always bode well for those who want to take the company to another level. In point of fact, the executive assumes everything is just fine, and after all, why would anyone in such an organization want to disrupt a good thing?

John Brown was part of the founding team of Lahood Plastics Corporation. He was one of those guys who saw the movie *The Graduate* in his last year of college and believed the line about the future being in plastics. After getting his early grooming and successes at a number of major chemical companies, he became part of a founding team of a divisional spin-off. Over the next few years as the business grew, Brown learned every aspect of the business, from operations through development, supply chain, and sales. Given the fact that Lahood Plastics was a spin-off of a major corporation and carried with it a great cash flow, it was not long before the company went public. Given his breadth of knowledge about the company and the company's steady performance, when the original CEO retired, as nominated and requested by the board of directors Brown stepped into the role of CEO and president and was in the role for fifteen years. During those fifteen years, Brown ran a good company: profitability was OK, market share was good, technology was steady, clients remained the same, and share price was stable. Lahood Plastics had simply always been a good company.

Robert Marley joined Lahood about three years ago. He came into the company in a business development capacity but quickly picked up all the operational aspects of the company, with a very keen interest in new technologies. Although he didn't graduate from a tier-one business school but instead a small liberal arts college, Marley had not only passion for business and technology but also considerable insight and talent. That enthusiasm extended to getting his arms around concepts like best practices, lean Six Sigma, and operational excellence. There was no question he had a positive impact on the company. Part of Marley's reason for joining Lahood was that he saw them as a company with great potential for moving into next-generation technology in plastics applications and manufacturing. John Brown had also been someone he had read about, and he was excited by the opportunity to work in his organization with someone who was a bit of a legend.

In the time he had been at Lahood, Marley realized that though Lahood had a great history and John Brown had a great legacy, the company was developing tremendous yet not fully realized vulnerabilities. The customers they were doing business with were only using Lahood's products for applications that were reaching end of life, while newer applications were being designed with materials from alternate suppliers. New competition was also emerging from nontraditional and international business. Although Brown had every right to feel proud of the quality and the performance of the product the company sold, the fact was that its manufacturing processes needed upgrading or replacement, and manufacturing costs needed to come down. Murmurs regarding these types of things had been going on for some time, but no one would ever take them to John Brown.

The problem was that Lahood Plastics was nearing a *strategic inflection point* in its business and was approaching a point where a "good" company was on the verge of become a "sort of good" company or "not a really bad" company. Unfortunately, even the board of directors were not seeing this. Board meetings had become nonchalant get-togethers because the board had come to accept the company's consistent performance and Brown's reliable hand on the helm. The board and the CEO were like Matt Dillon's Dodge City, except that the fiber of the town was eroding and no one was seeing it. Those who did would never challenge the marshal, and those who did challenge him found themselves out the door and on their way to "Boot Hill."

Very often, dodging bullets and shooting back comes down to choices that individuals make. In business, the options are straightforward: You leave the company and seek employment elsewhere, or you live with the status quo—after all, it's a safe company with low turnover, and you're assured of getting all the benefits customary with a stable job. You can try to effect change from within over time, but the chances of making a real impact in the reasonable future is unlikely. Lastly, you can approach the CEO and/or the board about initiating a new path, implementing a new idea, or developing a new product or market. At Lahood Plastics, Marley chose to try the last of these. After all, he did have a good reputation in the company, and he felt he had a reasonable chance of convincing Brown. He didn't, and the conversation went something like this:

Robert Marley: John, I have some great ideas that will help us grow market share, increase our profitability, and move us into newer and more dynamic markets.

John Brown: You know, Robert, you've done some very good things for the company, and I appreciate your creative ideas. Given the challenges and associated costs, why would I want to put a very good company at risk?

Robert Marley: That's the point, sir. The company is already at risk, and the market is beginning to see us as not being an innovative and dependable supplier in the future.

John Brown: Are you trying to convince me we have a problem here, because even our board is ecstatic about how the company is doing? Why, our performance for the past fifteen years has been excellent!

Robert Marley: Sir, I know the company has a fine history, but we can have a better future. Please don't be closed-minded about this.

John Brown: How dare you accuse me of being close-minded! Why, I am the reason this company is where it is today. I really thought you were a lot smarter than this, Marley, and I thought you had real loyalty to the company and to me.

Robert Marley: You're missing the point, sir.

John Brown: I'm not missing anything. What I am hearing is someone who has lost confidence in Lahood Plastics Corporation and now wants to disrupt a good thing. I don't want to hear any more about this this. Get out!"

Now, Marley's choice of words could be called into question in this discussion, but does anyone think the results would have been significantly different? Unlikely. Marley was now at a critical juncture with respect to his career at Lahood: should he continue to push back or begin polishing up his résumé? Marley didn't anticipate his actions would be perceived as calling the Marshal out, but in actuality, that's what he did. Now Robert could continue to press the issue. He could contact the board of directors, he could appeal to others in management, and he could reach out to clients. The simple truth is, he "drew" on the marshal, and in lightning speed he was put down and being carted off to the morgue.

The *Gunsmoke* scenario in some ways is a highly perplexing moment in the world of dodging bullets and shooting back. One would think that Robert Marley should have never had to dodge a bullet—after all, his intentions were positive and his approach was direct. But the corporate world is not always receptive to good advice and can create enemies very quickly and in unexpected ways. Top executives who are well-established and have a reasonably good corporate track record can take out almost anyone, because in their minds they will never be outdrawn. Whether the source of disruption and change is real or perceived, the marshals of this town are always going to win the personal and personnel battles—that is, until the town (company) succumbs to itself or other impacting market forces.

I have seen this scenario play out many times in Silicon Valley, and in some ways, I would say it has played out for the better. The innovation and the start-up environment most represented by Silicon Valley is truly a product of individuals who have stood up to the marshal when the marshal was wrong. Whether by choice or by termination, those individual who lost left the company. These same individuals were the ones who took their ideas and started their own firms. In time, many of these aggressive young start-ups overtook the marshal's company, and in some cases the start-up ended up acquiring the marshal's company. Then there are those ambitious young people who launched a start-up and ten years later resembled the marshal. There are many ways to shoot back, and becoming the competition is one of them.

CHAPTER 10

War Games: "M&A, Joint Ventures, Strategic Alliances, and Other Friendly Stuff"

> *All war is based on deception*
> —*Sun Tzu*

Tomorrow morning's headlines:

- Iran Pledges Cooperation in Its Acquisition of Iraq, Syria, Yemen, and Saudi Arabia
- China Supports United States/Russia Cooperation Initiative
- Apple and Samsung Form Strategic Alliance to Develop the I-Galaxy
- Walmart Announces Friendly Takeover of Target

Boy, don't these headlines sound really great! Iran will become the uniting benevolent force in the Middle East. The United States and Russia will now operate on a level playing field. Competition will end between Samsung and Apple, creating greater technology advancement. Everyone at Walmart and Target will maintain their positions in this "friendly" takeover. If you're buying one word of this, you've been living too long in Colorado and have a bit too much "Rocky Mountain high."

Now, these headlines may be exaggerations, but they're obviously meant to drive a point home. If you don't want to be a victim in the world of corporate deals, you'd better read beyond the headlines and see the writing on the wall. Change is coming, and it's going to be big. Have no doubt: someone is going to win, and "to the winner goes the spoils." The question is, where will you be when the war games begin, and are you prepared? The following two exchanges from the movie *WarGames* with Matthew Broderick say it all.

> *Joshua/WOPR*: Shall we play a game?
> *David*: Oh!
> *Jennifer*: I think it missed him.
> *David*: Yeah. Weird isn't it? Love to. How about Global Thermonuclear War.
> *Joshua/WOPR*: Wouldn't you prefer a good game of chess?
> *David*: Later. Right now let's play Global Thermonuclear War.
> *Joshua/WOPR*: Fine.

———

> *David*: What is the primary goal?
> *Joshua/WOPR*: You should know, Professor. You programmed me.
> *David*: Oh, c'mon. What is the primary goal?
> *Joshua/WOPR*: To win the game.

Most corporate strategists welcome a game of chess, with maybe a little more intrigue, but don't think for a minute that they are not playing "Global Thermonuclear War." In either case, the object of the game is to "win"! Bear in mind that sometimes even the designer(s) of the game don't really consider the consequences. All too often, the rules of the game change while the war is still being waged. The question is, after the war is over, how will they lead?

In the world of corporate mergers and acquisitions, all resources are put to work. The survivalist knows this and thinks and plans accordingly. The battle begins in advance of any deal being struck, and this holds to be truer when the deal is between competitors. Having no open hostilities does not mean that weapons aren't being deployed. Before, during, and after the war, assets are in use. Most of the types of shooters described in this book are engaged and reconnoitered to where they are required. It matters not which team you play for, as these assets will be used by both sides.

During my years working in the semiconductor industry, M&A activity, alliances, partnerships, and buyouts were ever present at an international level.

Whether culturally synergistic or culturally different, the methodology may have differed but the tools employed and the tactics used were essentially the same. I recall a deal being done in the Asia-Pacific region that involved two companies with complementary technologies. During that time period, it was not uncommon for manufactures to build their manufacturing base close to their competitor and in the same country, though sometimes in neighboring countries. The acquisition was thought to be a friendly one, where technology and manufacturing would be complementary and ultimately result in a stronger company.

Of course, anyone with any insight into the deal recognized that neither company alone, or as a result of a merger, could sustain the number of manufacturing sites that would result from the deal. Each company involved in the deal had product lines that had either reached the end of life or were simply no longer profitable. In addition, any joining of the companies would mean considerable redundancy in personnel, from management right down to the production floor. Prior to the deal even being finalized, each company was using its shooting assets to address headcount issues that were either negatively effecting the bottom line or simply could make the bottom line more attractive. The reality was, the act of dodging bullets would have been on full display within each company except that only the shooters knew who the targets were. Only the very savvy employees—or the ones who had experienced a similar takeover in the past—were figuring out how to dodge the forthcoming storm and, if necessary, position themselves for firing back. In some instances, the people actually doing the shooting would find that they had suddenly become targets as the battle moved into its latter stages.

In the first stage of this kind of transaction, leadership in each organization begins by assessing its own personnel. The team's perceived weak performers are weeded out by various types of shooters during this phase. This typically impacts those people sitting around "waiting to see what happens." This lack of proactivity is more than likely what made them a target in the first place and made them impotent when it came to dodging bullets. As a rule of thumb, many companies entering these types of transactions can quickly eliminate individuals by following the Jack Welch rule of eliminating the 10 percent lowest-performing individuals. Unfortunately, in an M&A deal, the performance criteria by which someone is measured can often be skewed. This is why knowing where you stands in the existing organization and scoping out your vision for yourself in the future organization is so critical. If you're waiting for someone to tell you what your new job is going to be, you probably don't have one.

Weakness or prior performance reviews are not the only reasons for an individual or a group to be singled out as a target. Stellar performers can easily become targets in these kinds of transactions. Those who are exceptional performers are almost always identified by existing management when ask by the other company's management who are standout individuals. These individuals may actually receive terrific accolades from their current employers, and they may in fact feel they are "bulletproof" when it comes to transitioning into the new company. As it will invariably happen, the executives of both companies will have a brief burst of enthusiasm as they identify these great performers and comment about their past successes and their future potential. If you listen to that part of the conversation, it is really exciting. One would immediately think that these individuals are the golden children and destined for great things. That is, until the next question: "How much is this person going to cost us?" Somehow, somewhere within the bowels of the due diligence being done, someone says, "Wow, this person is really expensive." A supportive manager might say, "But he or she is really good, and look at the contribution to the company." To which that manager hears again, "Wow, this person is really expensive." From that point on, the onslaught of follow-up questions begins: "Do we really need this person? Is she really necessary to achieve our plan? Don't we have someone else who can grow into that role and save us some money?" It goes on and on and on. The one-time revered performer has now become a piece of meat at the butcher, and someone is trying to decide whether they want a "prime cut" or will settle for "choice."

If the outstanding performer is truly outstanding, she will recognize that with the merger she has become a discretionary asset and that she should begin planning her own effort for dodging the bullet and launching a counterattack. It is difficult to say what type of shooter might be directed toward her, but if she is alert, she might be able to see the danger coming and dodge a bullet. Given her history, she might be able to see someone else get hit by a stray bullet, or there may be so much collateral damage around her that she emerges out of the rubble unscathed and all the wiser.

CHAPTER 11

COLLATERAL DAMAGE

Never has something so ordinary caused so much chaos...
—G. D. GEARINO, "DEALING WITH COLLATERAL
DAMAGE," *BUSINESS NORTH CAROLINA* (FEB. 2011)

I f there is one thing you don't want to ever be in the world of dodging bullets and shooting back, it's collateral damage. This, unfortunately, is easier said than done because most victims of collateral damage have little to no idea about what's going to befall them. Or do they? In fact, alleging that a victim of collateral damage is totally unaware is a half-truth. Collateral damage rarely occurs at the beginning of an engagement. In the workplace, an engagement can involve: a company hitting a strategic inflection point and changing course, an M&A event, the shutting down of a product line or corporate division, the sell-off of a product line or division, or simply a corporate restructuring. In most instances, the early targets and victims are clearly identified, with one or more shooters being deployed to address those specific individuals or groups. This is why implying that those who are collateral damage are blindsided is a half-truth. In the majority of instances, unless they've failed to pay attention, most victims of collateral damage understand that an engagement is in progress. Whether they believe they are insulated from the ramifications of that engagement is another story.

It is the standard scenario or naïveté of thinking that one is not directly involved in the fray that's taking place and therefore is allowed to go on with life as usual. This kind of thinking—let's say stupidity—might just get you killed in a professional sense. Fundamentally, in war, collateral damage is often the horrible price paid by innocent and not-so-innocent people who have been eliminated as the result of action taken by individuals who have a singular objective to eliminate a specific target, totally indiscriminate of others who might be injured or eliminated as part of achieving this goal. The corporate battlefield, however, is one place where people have a chance *not* to be collateral damage victims. Collateral damage is rarely singular in nature. It should never be confused with an individual taken down by a stray bullet, or a shooter who misses on his first shot and inadvertently takes someone else down. Collateral damage is significant when it happens, but it is not unavoidable. Don't become collateral damage.

How often have we seen this played out in the real world of business and politics? Once a person becomes collateral damage, he can never fully recover and what recovery is available to him is not typically worth pursuing. Take the case of Samsa Corporation. This twenty-year-old business that produced antibacterial agents had reached a critical juncture in its corporate evolution. Run by a very smart and intuitive management team, the company realized it needed to restructure and redirect its business in order to keep pace with the industry, reduce costs, mitigate risks, and increase overall profitability. The company's intention was to make the kind of changes that would support a go-forward strategy in order to secure the long-term viability of the company—an effort fully supported by the board of directors and shareholders.

Daniel Berretta and Justin Ceebiyu, CEO and CFO respectively, had done a tremendous amount of planning in preparation for the changes they would be putting forth in the company. They had met for weeks with department heads and outside advisers, including a human resources specialist, to ensure their plan could be executed expediently. The lowest-performing individuals in the company had been identified, executives who would not be part of the strategic change process were already listed, and different types of shooters had been enlisted to "address their futures." A great deal of uncertainty existed within the workforce as to how widespread the changes would be, and the reactions in the company ranged from those who were panic-stricken, to those who were going with the flow, to those who were already either playing politics inside the company or sprucing up their résumés for their departure.

Some departments, like Gordon Brewster's, were feeling secure and were prepared to move forward. Individually, Gordon, the VP of business operations, was an excellent performer and ran a good organization. He group-supported several product lines and delivered consistent performances. Gordon had already begun thinking about how his team of fifteen would meld into the new organizational structure and what their deliverables would be to the company. Although two of the product lines Gordon's group supported were destined to wind down, he was already clear, at least to himself, about where his group would fill in and continue to contribute.

Unknown to Gordon, Daniel and Justin had already nailed down their strategy for all departments and all product lines, as well as how they wanted those groups to run and who they wanted to run them. Daniel and Justin were fully aware of Gordon's excellent performance and saw him as a critical tool with respect to the company's future. As part of their strategy, they were going to combine two divisions and elevate Brewster to the position of senior VP. This move was designed to specifically cut costs and enhance profits. The shedding of old product lines and the merging of complementary product lines would allow the new division to act like a start-up and build a strong and viable business over time. Given that the new division would be operating in start-up mode, and given that Gordon's division had fifteen people while the other former division had twenty-five, and given that the new division required only twelve staff people to launch, there was bound to be collateral damage.

When Gordon was called in to see Daniel and Justin and they announced to him his new title and responsibility, he was elated, recognizing that he had been targeted for success and had not only dodged a bullet but was advancing in the corporation's leadership ranks. In that same moment, he realized there would be a collateral impact to his being targeted for a promotion. His fifteen longtime loyal and productive staff members would have to be merged with the twenty-five-member staff of the other division and then cut back to twelve. Until this point in time, Brewster's people had been feeling extremely secure and were counting on him to present their next challenge. In an instant, Brewster had gone from being a target to a shooter, but those around him and those in the other division had become collateral damage. In Gordon's meeting with Daniel and Justin, they had worked it out that six members of each division would remain with the new organization. In a flash, twenty-eight people found themselves packing up their desks and heading into the sunset. Could any of them have prevented themselves from becoming collateral damage? The answer is possibly, but it takes commitment to knowing your business as well if not better than those who are running it.

We started this section by suggesting that people in the workplace can't really prevent themselves from becoming collateral damage and then calling this a half-truth. If you live in a war zone, you should have an expectation of being collateral damage. The same applies for businesses in transition. In war zones, people see their friends and neighbors, along with complete strangers, become collateral damage. It cannot possibly be a surprise when bombs are dropping all around you and you see others fall. Having an expectation of becoming collateral damage when you are part of a business in transition should not only be anticipated but should be considered probable. Once you have that level of understanding, you no longer have to question the thought processes behind every executive decision being made; you should rather be considering and planning your next move before the damage heads in your direction. This is not to say you will not be wounded, but it will ensure you never become a serious casualty. Yes, you may still lose your position with the company, but if you have an expectation of that possibility, you can certainly have alternatives readied in order to keep you moving forward. Collateral damage may be inevitable in some situations, but no one says you need to be its victim.

CHAPTER 12

DRONE STRIKE: OF DRONES AND DROIDS

It is not the strongest species that survives, nor the most intelligent, but the ones most responsive to change.
—CHARLES DARWIN

What's that buzzing sound I hear? *Bam, boom, crash!* It's not "Star Wars," and it ain't no video game! In fact, if you're still playing "Star Wars," the war was lost before it even began. Ever think that the *bam, boom, and crash* sound is the last sound a terrorist or an enemy hears before "holy hell" falls upon him or her? You'd be wrong. By the time those sounds are heard, the terrorist is already dead. The last sound the terrorist hears is a soft droning sound and then perhaps a whistling sound just before being eliminated. It's a weapons-loaded drone, which in the wink of an eye can take out an individual or group of individuals. It also occasionally results in something we discussed earlier: collateral damage. It's the technology of war, and it's everywhere.

Drones are not just unmanned long-range weapons. They come from the development of sophisticated technologies that are superior to anything our enemies have considered and are unable to defend against. It is truly a faceless weapons system with the capability of bringing down individuals, armies, regimes, and possibly countries. It is the war that some might say is won "not with a boom, but a click."

In business, let alone in life, technology has proven to be both a tool of good and a weapon of evil. If you're an enemy, technology can wreak havoc on you. If you control the technology, you can anticipate many victories.

In the right hands, technology has the capability of bringing so much good to the world. Consider the advances in science, medicine, and the mobile networks that keep us all connected. In the wrong hands, it creates chaos, hardship, pain, and failure. Look at the software-related viruses we are infected by because of unnamed and faceless hackers whose only objective is to create digital anarchy. If you learn about technology, use it, and integrate it into your world, it becomes fantastic tool and makes you less vulnerable, particularly on the corporate battlefield. If you or your company fail to keep up with it, you are not only left at the figurative station, but you probably didn't even know there was a train. In the corporate world, whether you are an individual or a corporation, technology can eliminate your existence or give you an incredible edge. Technology is a bullet shot with a silencer that comes with blinding speed and accomplishes exactly what the shooter wants. You'd better have it in your arsenal, be prepared to use it, and certainly learn how to dodge it, but most importantly you should never ignore it.

This book would be incomplete if I did not take the time to address the essence of technology. The drone metaphor simply emphasizes the point that wars are won, not based on the size of one's military, but on the technical sophistication of one's arsenal and the knowledge of how to use the tools that have been developed. In almost any corporate or company environment and in almost any industry, technology is ever present. It touches you and your business, whether you are on Wall Street or Main Street. There are many ways to be taken out by technology, and it can hit you whether you are an employee in a company, the owner of the company, or the actual company. The average person today thinks of technology in terms of her mobile device, tablet, and notebook PC, unless through her profession or personal life she is exposed to other forms of technology. Silicon Valley and the tech industry worldwide illustrate the rubble of companies that once were and are no longer because they failed to stay more than a step ahead of their competitors. Like the Red Queen said to Alice as they were running through the forest: "To get anywhere you need to run twice as fast."

We have to remember that we've not been invaded by new technologies, new instruments, and new machines; we've developed them, and there does not appear to be any end to their proliferation. In most instances, we've developed these for the common good. The advancement in medicine has been phenomenal. Patients in hospitals and physicians' offices are exposed to life-saving innovation routinely. Our ability to communicate and travel across the globe both physically and virtually has opened up markets and improved relationships with countries, cities, and people around the world. We have been able to drive a vehicle across the surface of Mars and look into the deepest reaches of the galaxy. Patients can get new or artificial organs, and our overall life expectancy has risen considerably. We can see a great movie and in a "click" tell our ten thousand closest friends about it. And we can text the friend sitting across from us how good our hamburger is without ever looking at him. Yes, technology is a wondrous thing.

Although human beings may have developed technology, we are anything but bulletproof to it, and like us, the technology we've developed is itself not bulletproof. Dodging bullets and shooting back takes on an entirely different dimension and is far more complex when it comes to technology. Technologies can compete and fire upon themselves in the form of corporate competition and acquisitions. Two or more different technologies often go after the same end market but follow different paths. How often do we see this? Look at the life cycle of music mediums from vinyl to digital and a similar cycle for visual media. Consider medicine at a time when the only way to learn the extent of a disease or treat a disease was through some invasive procedure or some even more barbaric method. Now we can determine a treatment or even a cure for some diseases without physically seeing the patient. Examine the rise of the commercial space program, and again there are competing technologies. The fastest to the draw may win on the streets of Tombstone, but in the world of technology, it is the one who uses fast development cycle times to meet a market demand who lives to breathe another day. The click of a computer key has replaced the click of the handgun's hammer, with far more devastating results.

The life expectancy of a technology is substantially shorter than the life expectancy of a human in the majority of instances. This is all the more reason why companies and individuals need to understand the technological ecosystem in which they reside and at the same time be cognizant of technologies that exist outside their sphere. Now, some might argue that we still have TVs, radios, refrigerators, and other familiar appliances, but actually these are far different technologies than you knew as a child or your parents used. The examples of this are unending. People talk about the species of life that become extinct every day. Well, we can safely say that technologies become extinct every day as new technologies evolve and old ones fade away or just die, while others never make it through the gestation period.

> *It is not necessary to change. Survival is not mandatory.*
> —*W. Edwards Deming*

Many a company has failed either because of its inability to keep pace with technology or due to its inability to deploy innovative technology. There are so many companies that have failed in the lab because they were looking for the perfect solution as opposed to providing the solution people wanted and they already had. Individuals have learned that the inability to keep up with technology can be a detriment to their advancement and sometimes lead to their company eliminating their job and them completely. This is applicable in any industry. Beyond this, however, there is a more sinister element, which like our drone strike simile can be devastating both corporately and personally.

Corporately, personally, and governmentally, the real drone strikes and true war games are taking place in cyberspace. Whether in the form of hardware or software, these attacks can be launched at an individual or a group, and they do not discriminate. They are specifically designed to be disruptive, create chaos, and leave their victims stunned and defeated. We are under attack, and the current prognosis is that things will get worse long before they get better. Dodging these attacks is an illusion, as we are in fact only creating false barriers of protection that can easily be overrun. How safe are you and your company from these attacks? Not very! If you haven't experienced the panic of a virus invading your personal PC, you've been lucky so far. The experience of seeing everything on your computer screen disappear in front of your eyes as some malevolent hacker destroys your work and your files in a flash is well beyond disruptive. Even worse is when you show up at your ATM and your account has been drained or your store credit card has been maxed out and you haven't made a purchase at that store in weeks. Suddenly, your own vulnerability to a "drone strike" (cyberattack) staggers you because you have neither the tools nor the wherewithal to shoot back at this type of attack.

Your own vulnerability and lack of ability to protect yourself doesn't seem so bad when you hear all the corporate horror stories. No sooner do you finish saying "Why me?" or "How could this happen?" when you hear stories out of the media: "Target Gets Hacked; Millions of Retail Customers Compromised," or "Home Depot Reports Hackers Disrupted Their Systems," or "Hackers Have Stolen More Than Tens of Millions of Personal Data Files from the IRS." WikiLeaks! Even Hillary Clinton! If our own government can't protect itself from these "drone strikes," how do we protect ourselves and our companies? For the moment, through a combination of mesh screens and Band-Aids. If there is a solution, it will be found in the private sector, while in the near term we continue to press governments to ensure that when they uncover these people, they prosecute to the fullest extent of the law. Despite the wonderment and the convenience of some technology, when it goes wrong, it not only fails us, but it joins the other side. The unanswered question is, "What can we do about it?"

The answer, whether you are a corporation or an individual, is to be proactive. There are a lot of things in business where counterpunching works, but not with technology. At the individual level, don't be intimidated by what you don't know. If you're a corporation, again, don't be intimidated by what you don't know. Find the most knowledgeable and effective individuals you can to train both you and your staff. Keep abreast of where the cutting-edge technologies are and how those technologies can affect your business. Engage in technology benchmarking from within your industry and businesses outside your industry. Innovative technologies, when understood and used properly, can actually be the best tool for dodging bullets before the gun is in the shooter's hand.

Technology is a tool through which humans demonstrate their desire for advancement for the betterment of our species. Technology is a weapon by which humans surpass their enemies and their competition in order to exert dominance over an individual, a specific industry, or possibly over the entire world. Who are the individuals developing technology, and how do you learn about the technology threats of which you currently have no knowledge? What is the purpose behind that technology? The intent may not be malicious at all but rather the evolution of an existing technology, or it may be the disruptive force of a revolutionary technology. Disruptive technologies are only disruptive to those who did not anticipate or search for them. Only if you fail to embrace new technology will that technology become disruptive.

CHAPTER 13

RUSSIAN ROULETTE: FOR ONE

*"I have a very strict gun control policy: if there's
a gun around, I want to be in control of it."*
—CLINT EASTWOOD

The easiest bullet to dodge and the most challenging bullet to dodge is the one aimed at your head when you're holding the gun. This is the bullet that can only be fired by an act of personal choice and one where only you can be accountable, no matter what the factors were leading up to it. Any suggestion that the gun went off by accident is nothing more than self-deceit. The trigger can be pulled for a plethora of reasons, which include but are not limited to: stupidity, self-sacrifice, more stupidity, martyrdom, even greater stupidity, heroism, complete and utter stupidity, and carelessness. Does anyone really want to pull the trigger on a gun in this position? Isn't this really the point of Clint Eastwood's quote above? When the gun is in your hand, you become the decision maker, you are in control, and you decide where to aim it and who to aim it at, so why point it at yourself? Business is a lot of things, but it is not the Russian roulette scene from the movie *The Deer Hunter.*

I don't doubt for a moment that if you ask yourself to come up with the names of corporate leaders, politicians, sports stars (sports is a business), celebrities, and even business associates who have all put bullets in their heads, you could rattle off ten or twenty in a matter of seconds. Only in extremely rare cases can someone fully recover from a self-inflicted gunshot wound. When we see someone who has committed professional suicide or at least gone as far as to severely injure himself or herself, there is one of three utterances we hear from people. The first is: "Oh shit!" The second is: "Why would they do that?" The third is: "I knew it!" There is always an answer, and there are also those who choose to disbelieve or make excuses. There are those who wonder where the shooter got the gun and why it was picked up, and there are those who saw the gun in the person's hand and instead of shouting, "Put down the gun," simply remained silent. On occasion there are those who see the shooter holding the gun, see it aimed at their head, and at that moment are screaming for the person to put the gun down. This, unfortunately, is not typical. Whatever the case, there is only one person pulling the trigger, and only that person is behind the choice to do so. So as a refresher course in business suicide and self-inflicted wounds, let's take a look at some of the ways this happens.

How is it that when we think of corporate or political suicide, our brains move immediately from our head to our genitals? (Yes, I've even included sex in this book). In the next few paragraphs, I'll discuss the various ways in which people take themselves out in the business and political world, but sex is usually at the top of the list. Poor performance may not always constitute a decision to do poorly, but sex always involves a conscious decision. There was a time when women thought they could "screw" themselves up the corporate ladder and men thought being at the top of the ladder entitled them to have sex within anyone they chose and without repercussions. How many leaders, corporate and otherwise, have grabbed their gun and put it in the wrong place? This is not gender specific by any means; the weapon of choice is simply made differently and used differently. The clichés have been around for generations: "Don't put your hand in the company cookie jar." In the newer *Mad Men* age of business, we've added, *"And don't become the company cookie jar,"* even if it's only for one hand. If corporate sexual scandals were only driven by innuendos, individuals might in time overcome them, but typically they're not. The fact is, from the executive suite to the Oval Office, and from the mail room to the company parking lot, executives and employees for generations have been putting guns to their heads and pulling the trigger.

Whether an individual engages in an ongoing corporate romance or a wild one-night fling, "messing around" with peers, subordinates, or superiors is not only a bad idea, but it can also be fatal. The only exception to this rule might be if you are the president of the United States playing around with a twenty-something intern. (I by no means intend to get into politics in this book, and I don't want to reenact the entire Bill Clinton/Monica Lewinsky story. I do, however, want to use it as an example.) Picture a ten-billion-dollar company, or for that matter, a ten-million-dollar company. Now imagine that as part of its policy, the company invites college interns to join it every summer for the purpose of seeking potential candidates for the future, and to provide an opportunity for the interns to experience life in the corporate world. The company is run by a highly visible CEO. (This would apply whether it's simply someone visible in his town or county, or someone who is high profile on the national stage.) Either way, this person has achieved a level of recognition within his economic and social ecosystem. As is the company's practice on the first day of orientation for the summer interns, the CEO has lunch with the interns and gives a small speech about the company, its vision for the future, and the importance of the summer intern program to that future. During his speech, the CEO, a man noted for his high character and principles, notices an attractive young woman staring at him intently, smiling and hanging on to every word he says. When the speech is over and the staff and interns are mixing it up, the infatuated young woman comes up and speaks with the CEO. Her tone is enthusiastic, effervescent, and highly flirtatious, almost to the point where the CEO feels he is back in college. Of course, he is not in college, and his wife and two kids at home are clear proof of that. Over the course of the next month, the young intern spends considerable time stopping by the CEO's office, asking lots of questions about the business, making light humor, and occasionally making casual physical contact.

The CEO begins to finds himself participating in this flirtation and focuses very hard on not letting it extend beyond anything but flirtation. That is, until he is working late one night and a head pops in to see how he's doing. It's the college intern. There is no need to go into details as to what takes place, and in fact, it takes place with a moderate amount of frequency over the next couple of months. The CEO doesn't ever really reconcile with himself what caused them to step across the line, nor did he care very much during these interludes. His brain had already made the physiological shift. The twenty-one-year-old intern was enamored with this man, twenty-eight years her senior, and would do anything he asked of her.

Company rumors run rampant, and it becomes very hard for the pair to cover up their flirtatious affair. Getting caught was inevitable and certainly something for which the CEO should have been fully prepared. Whether it was arrogance or stupidity, he succumbed. He could have had no idea that the little out-of-the-way beach hotel he checked into with the intern was having a charity luncheon on the same day—in which, as it so happened, one of his board member's wife was a participant. The meeting of this woman, the intern, and the CEO was, at its best, awkward. Let it suffice to say that from that point on things began to unravel and word spread to the board, through the company, and to the CEO's family.

The reality is that there are no social secrets when it comes to an office. The professional and public outcry are deafening when it comes to calling for the CEO's resignation. His history of running a highly profitable and successful business is dismissed. His alleged excellent integrity, which until now has never been questioned, and his recognized philanthropy to the community are totally eradicated. A forty-nine-year-old married man with a twenty-one-year-old intern carrying on in the office and "God knows where else" becomes a monster, a male chauvinist pig, and a pathetic human being, and each of those comments are preceded with an expletive starting with "f" and ending with "ing." This would not and cannot stand. From the day the CEO engaged in a flirtatious encounter with the intern, he was holding the gun to his head. He had the option to throw the gun away or pull the trigger. He chose the latter and with that choice took down his own career. Unless you're the president of the United States or run a business elsewhere in the world where this behavior might be tolerated, maybe France, your chances of surviving this type of suicidal action is near impossible. Only if you're president of the United States does the woman get blamed.

Corporate suicide via lust is not the only way individuals are eliminated by putting the gun to their head. As we said earlier, it is always a choice, with some choices being much clearer than others. The reason for clarity or lack thereof can often be associated with risk. Projects, business deals, mergers, new clients, new technology, new suppliers, and fundamentally any decision that could result in a change in how a business runs present risks. There are real risks and there are perceived risks, and ironically the real risks always have more clarity than the perceived ones. Real risks are based on facts or a combination of results that provide "either/or" scenarios. These tend to be far more objective. Perceived risks become more subjective and play very much to an individual or group's state of mind and personal or group prejudices. Perceived risk has very little in the way of certainty because of the emotional component. Oddly enough, those operating based on perceived risk believe they have far more clarity, when in point of fact they don't. A course of action for a company based on "real" risks can be executed because the associated decision has quantifiable information and data to provide a meaningful level of support, and although there is no certainty in this scenario, there is a great deal of clarity.

Following our "dodging bullets, shooting back" concept, when an individual has to make a critical decision, whether risk is perceived or real, the gun is always going to be in that individual's hand. The result of pulling the trigger lies with the subsequent series of events. The weapon may be loaded with live ammo, or it could be loaded with blanks. Either way, when the individual is you pulling the trigger, you will live or die based on your decision. Although this is not Russian roulette, it is about as close to it as we can get in the corporate world. The risk component of "perceived or real" is only a determinate of how many bullets are in the gun. Executives, managers, bosses, and leaders of all kinds, depending on the organization they operate, find themselves with the gun pressed against their temple more often than you might think over the course of their career. Some occasionally get lucky by shooting themselves in the foot, and that injury becomes a lesson and a factor in their future decision-making methodology. It's like the executive who makes a significant but not unrecoverable error that costs her company a significant amount of money. The executive believes this mistake will assuredly end her career and as a result prepares a letter of resignation. When the CEO learns of the forthcoming resignation, he is furious, stating, "How dare she quit! Do you realize what it's cost to train her?" We've all heard this type of story in the past. IBM's founder Tom Watson comes to mind, and it is definitely applicable to executives who are capable of learning from their mistakes. Sometimes shooting yourself in the foot saves you from the greater error of shooting yourself in the head.

In some cases of corporate suicide, the choice is really an existential one. There are many scenarios where organizational absurdities reach all-time highs. Unfortunately, there are many highly dysfunctional companies. Many are listed on the NYSE or NASDAQ; others are privately held or family owned. The size of the company can sometimes be directly correlated with the size of its dysfunctionality. This is mostly because there are more moving parts in a large corporation, so there are more areas for people and structures to break down. Large corporations, because of their size, have the financial sustaining power that small companies don't when it comes to dysfunctionality. In these dysfunctional environments, chaos and failure abound, from the boardroom to the lunchroom. Even if the dysfunction is taking place at the very top of the organization, the ripple effect is widespread. When this happens, any individual in the company may actually end up pulling the trigger.

Savvy business executives have a tough time with executing decisions they know are wrong. When they find themselves in a Sisyphus-type situation, the choice does not have to be the perpetual pushing of the boulder up the hill only to see it roll down again. They also do not have to choose self-annihilation as it relates to their professional life. As we will see in the "dodging bullets" section of this book, there is a way to survive, even when you put the gun to your head and pull the trigger. This adds a slightly different twist to the concept of holding a gun to one's head. Businesspeople who find they're in this type of situation realize that time is not their friend and that sooner or later a shooter will be coming for them or their bosses, or in other instances, they will get caught in a cluster f—k. So given the options, keeping control in their own hands is the absolute right choice.

This is also true of martyrdom. There are corporate situations where an individual realizes that by taking himself out of the equation he can save the jobs of others and possibly the entire corporation.

> *I have learned to love that which is meant to harm me, so*
> *that I can stand in the way of those who are less strong.*
> *I can take the bullets for those who aren't able to.*
> —Margaret Cho

In these instances, the individual is more than likely one of the strongest performers in the company, if not part of company leadership. This is not an easy decision for one to make, but the wise individual will know to make it. I recall once taking an executive management course at Harvard Business School. During one of the sessions where the discussion was around executive insight, a woman executive from a major utility company indicated that her firm had a new CEO and that this CEO said he lived by the three "Ls": look, learn, and listen. Having no desire to lessen the woman's expectations of her new CEO, I did however have to intercede and say that if her new boss was truly a visionary leader, he would live by the four "Ls": look, learn, listen, and leave. How one chooses to exit a company may be greater than the decision to join a company. The ability to comprehend this will prove to be one of the most important rules to remember when it comes to dodging bullets and shooting back.

SECTION II

DODGING BULLETS

Neo: "What are you trying to tell me?
That I can dodge bullets?"
Morpheus: "No, Neo. I'm trying to tell you that
when you're ready, you won't have to."
—THE MATRIX

CHAPTER 14

How Not to Be a Target

I never saw the shooter, nor heard the gunshot, but in my being I felt the bullet coming straight for me, and I dodged it.
—HARRY ROZAKIS

Did you ever wonder why some people are always able to dodge a bullet? Ever think about why some people never even have to dodge bullets? What about those peoples who seem to be endlessly in the cross hairs of someone's weapon? What is so different about these people? There are many who would attribute it to luck, both good and bad. Now, I don't deny that there can be an element of luck in any situation, but I believe when it comes to dodging bullets and shooting back there is always evidence to follow. I would also assert that although luck is a factor on occasion, in actuality intuitiveness, intelligence, knowledge, wisdom, and the quick thinking on the part of a prospective target and those around her is what keeps the so-called lucky ones alive and moving forward.

The conversation between Morpheus and Neo in the movie *The Matrix* might be the most important lesson in this book. In the workplace, in politics, and in life there are always battles being waged and bullets being fired. The entire premise of this book is our earlier quote: "The best time to dodge a bullet is before the gun is in the shooter's hand." This is essentially what Morpheus is telling Neo. In the earlier chapters, we listed and described some of the types of shooters and various ways one can be "taken out" in the workplace. None of these shooters, nor their methodologies, is exactly the same. The figurative shooters in the business world did not start their careers by carrying a gun. This is critical to understand, because in business there is sometimes a false assumption that the people who will take you out are the ones who are already toting a gun. They're not! Shooters emerge out of a multitude of corporate situations, and just because an individual has never been a shooter doesn't mean he or she can't learn. For some, it's a learned talent driven by a need; for others, it's a skill that comes natural. Some go into business knowing they need protection in advance; others do it to help their companies survive. This is why it is so critical to be able to identify shooters and in some cases identify them before they think about becoming one.

What causes one to become a target? This is something you've probably questioned as you've read this book. If you know the answer to this, it is a big stride toward at least being able to dodge a bullet and at best ensure that not only are you never fired upon, but no one would ever think of firing at you. There are many things that make individuals targets, and understanding as many of these things as quickly as possible is the first step in understanding how to dodge bullets. No one has to be a victim on the corporate battlefield. Factors that contribute to becoming a victim include but are not limited to: fear, stupidity, carelessness, denial, poor performance, laziness, lack of commitment, and other similar behaviors. When weighing these characteristics, *fear* outweighs all others. I am sure there are some who will read this and say, "No, it's got to be stupidity, not fear." This is a debate I am ready to have at any time. To use the old adage, "You can't cure stupid." Stupidity can be an issue of someone refusing or not caring to be informed. Stupid is a product of being out of touch, of just not caring, or yes, of just being *stupid*.

No matter your intellect, fear can be instilled in almost any individual. It is managing fear that determines how a person dodges a bullet or, for that matter, ensures he or she never has to dodge a bullet. Fear grips people in many ways and is triggered by many things. When people become fearful, those people tend to retreat, hide, take cover, or break down. When fear strikes in business, it makes no difference whether you run a "Ma and Pop" shop or a publicly traded company.—it becomes totally disruptive. Fear, if not managed, can be all consuming. It can take the highest to the lowest, the strongest to the weakest, and the richest to the poorest. It does not discriminate. The small business owner can worry about covering bills, making payroll, paying taxes, and satisfying stakeholders. The CEO of a giant corporation shares these same fears in most instances. For many, fear comes when they are confronted with a problem they perceive as being fundamentally unsolvable, a problem they perceive as shattering their career or their company. Fear is exasperating and debilitating, and can manifest itself physically as well as mentally.

In the corporate world, fear will makes you a soft target. Performance and results are often encumbered as a result of fear, and this also facilitates one becoming a target. Decision making becomes skewed when one is fearful and becomes more about preservation than leadership. The person who is constantly fretting about his job perpetuates himself as a target and then is consumed with the fear of being a target. In leadership, those who are constantly worried about what their board thinks, their shareholders think, or the public thinks can succumb to fear and destroy themselves by constantly engaging in second-guessing.

I once heard the motivational speaker Anthony Robbins say that FEAR is an acronym, standing for *False Evidence that Appears Real.* The real-life Neos never have to dodge a bullet because not only have they made fear a tool they can use, but they have turned it into an ally. They have readjusted how they think and react to it. Instead of being a negative trigger, fear becomes a positive trigger in that it sets off a reaction that demands one to think smarter, act wiser, and move quicker. When you remove fear as a possibility, you also remove failure as a possibility. In business, you have to embrace fear if you're going to avoid ever becoming a target. Turn fear into the motivating force that drives, productivity, success, and ultimately survival. Follow the history of corporate giants throughout history: Vanderbilt, Rockefeller, Morgan, Ford, Watson, Grove, Jobs, Gates, etc. How many of them stood on the precipice of doom and ruin? It was their fear that generated the decision not to fail. Adopt this philosophy, and you may never have to dodge a bullet.

> *One who fears failure limits his activities. Failure is*
> *only the opportunity to more intelligently begin again.*
> —HENRY FORD

One can't consciously dodge a bullet by being stupid, although I don't believe anyone would argue that we've seen many stupid people dodging bullets without being cognizant of the fact that they were ever someone's target. We've seen other stupid people who should be at the top of the target list and yet they unwittingly never even make the list. When it happens, most of us are in total disbelief. Let me quote Forest Gump: "Stupid is as stupid does." When stupid survives, it goes unaddressed because either no one sees it for what it is, or it is simple dismissed as "being stupid" because the target is fundamentally irrelevant to the shooter, who has much bigger game to go after. This, however, is the exception, and it is rare in the corporate world that stupid goes unnoticed. Sometimes there are those who are left as a later target because they are so easy to take out. If you're smart enough to think about acting stupid, you're smart enough to dismiss any thought of it immediately. Your brain was meant to do more important things, as we will soon illustrate.

Many of those who find they are in the sights of a shooter will never dodge a bullet, because even though they are cognizant of everything taking place in their company, they live in a world of denial. Denial and refusal are essentially the same thing when it comes to not being able to dodge a bullet. Those who are taken out because they deny the events taking place around them typically have the intellect to appreciate that they could become a corporate victim, but they unfortunately create stories and a belief system that for a while insulates them from the truth. The longer this process takes, the more vulnerable those individuals become. Over the years I have seen quite a number of people take the path of denial. In many cases, they've been part of large corporations like IBM, GE, Citigroup, and a number of others, including major Wall Street firms. In some instance, these people had put more than twenty years in with the firm. These were people whose fathers worked in the firm, or they currently had siblings and spouses working in the firm. In all these situations, there was a "this will never happen to me" kind of attitude. With this kind of attitude, all the body armor in the world will not protect you. I have seen founders and longtime CEOs who had convinced themselves that they were invulnerable to market and corporate Armageddon. I have witnessed instances where the shooters have actually telegraphed their next move to these people and still they remained in denial. Denial is essentially a death wish, and if you ever hope to dodge a bullet, you need to remove *denial* from your vocabulary.

Shooters always look for vulnerabilities. If you are tasked with being a shooter, in addition to fear, stupidity, and denial, you are going to look for things like carelessness, poor performance, laziness, and lack of commitment by an individual or group. If you're an employee who has exhibited any of these characteristics, you'd better realize that someone is going to come gunning for you. If you are a corporate group or division, and your organization shows evidence of this kind of behavior, you will be hunted down. If you're naive enough to believe that this will not happen, then you fall into the denial category. Even if you're one of these people, it doesn't mean you can't dodge bullets. The first rule is to recognize that the behavior that took you to the point of having to dodge a bullet is not the behavior that will work when you're actually dodging that bullet. Survival is a huge motivator, and I have seen individuals who have truly dodged a bullet because they changed and used some of the techniques we'll speak about later. There are no assurances that you will survive if you change your behavior, but one thing is for sure: if you don't make the effort, you don't stand a chance. Let's face it: if you've been lazy on the job, apathetic, demonstrated a lack of commitment to projects and deadlines, or failed to play as part of a team, then you've basically been holding the gun to your head for some time. And since you don't have the commitment to take yourself out of a situation, you're waiting for someone else to do it for you. Let me be clear that this does not just happen to people who are lazy; it also happens to people who become disenfranchised because, though really talented, they are put into a position where they are extremely unhappy—and in order to try and be a good soldier and tough it out, they stay in the position and do nothing, including not bringing it to the attention of their superiors. If you're one of these people, as we'll highlight in the "shooting back" section of this book, sometimes you just need to leave town.

Now that we've talked about those things that can cause you to become a target, let's address the different methods for dodging bullets. As Morpheus again points out, once you know how to dodge bullets, you will not have to. Mitigating your chance of being a target is a good start. So how is this done? The argument can be made that the way to ensure you never put yourself in the position of being a target is to work hard, be a stellar performer, and tow the corporate line. Though there is some rationale here, it simply isn't the truth. The in-your-face truth is that you are expendable. No matter what your position, you can be replaced. This happens to owners, CEOs, and investors who truly believe they are invulnerable, and it happens more often than you may think. Accepting responsibility for your own vulnerability is what will save your life. CEOs who have risen through the ranks know this better than anyone. They have spent their careers maneuvering through the company, and probably somewhere along the line, they set it up so that a shooter took out a rival, allowing them to move into the next slot. Are they bad guys for doing this? Hell, no! They are doing what is necessary, and if the performance of their department or the company is exceptional, then they must be doing something right. The same holds true for those CEOs who step into a company but from the outset establish their timeline for an exit. As we've said earlier, knowing when to leave is a key component of never having to dodge a bullet.

CHAPTER 15

DODGING TECHNIQUES: ONLY CATS HAVE NINE LIVES

I know what you're thinking. "Did he fire six shots or only five?" Well to tell you the truth in all this excitement I kinda lost track myself. But being this is a 0.44 Magnum, the most powerful handgun in the world and would blow your head clean off, you've gotta ask yourself one question: "Do I feel lucky?" Well, do ya, punk?
—CLINT EASTWOOD AS HARRY CALLAHAN, DIRTY HARRY

Well, "do you feel lucky?" If your answer is yes, then don't bother reading any further because you're stuck in denial and there is not much the rest of this book can do for you. Looking down the barrel of a 0.44 Magnum, even figuratively, means you've made a great number of seriously poor decisions. After having five or maybe six shots headed in your direction in your professional life and coming to find that you are still looking down the barrel of a gun, you've gotta ask yourself one question: "Do I feel stupid?" Well do ya, punk? How many lives do you actually think you have?

Cats are quick, cunning, and predatory creatures, and so it is said that they have nine lives. Those same characteristics attributable to cats having nine lives can at times be the same reason they need them. Moving too quick, being too cunning, and even being a predator can use up a lot of lives very quickly. During a professional career, you have many opportunities for second chances, but within a given company you have one life and you'd best know how to protect it. Learning how to dodge bullets is the first step in never having to dodge one.

71

Although there are many instances where being a shooter is justifiable, letting yourself be the target on the other end of the barrel without recourse is foolish. As we said earlier, the first rule of thumb is: "trust no one." Come to accept the fact that people can betray you. This does not mean they *will* betray you, and it doesn't mean they will necessarily do it over something big. Despite perceived kindness and friendship, even the most trustworthy, honest individual you know in the entire world can at some point betray you for some petty reason. If self-interest is involved, anyone can justify an act of betrayal. Does this mean you should hate everyone or steer clear of people? Of course not. What it really means is, don't be disappointed when they do betray you. Self-preservation is a human instinct, and at some point in time every individual you know will disappoint you in some way. And it's OK.

One man's perception of betrayal is another man's perception of a winning negotiation. When negotiating corporate deals, there are always shooters at the table. Some wear corporate hats, some juggle numbers, and some use the ambivalence that exists in the law to arm their team. How many times in a corporate negotiation or M&A scenario has at least one party come forward and said, "What we're looking for here is a win/win situation"? Unfortunately, win/win is about perceptions, not reality. It's about the shooters on the other side of the table trying to change the other side's perception of win/win so they can keep their guns holstered. If the side manipulating the perception is successful, then they can affirm to themselves that there was no betrayal involved because the other side came to understand the deal. Win/win always has a win/lose component, but it is never seen until reality eliminates one side's perception. The bullet of changing perception is one that is always used in negotiations. It is imperative that when your team is negotiating a transaction, they are prepared to dodge this bullet before it is ever fired. Call it manipulation, betrayal, or simply changing perceptions, the technique will always be used, even in negotiations allegedly striving for a perceived win/win outcome.

Dodging bullets mean being alert and not allowing half-truths and lies to seduce you into not being prepared for what's about to be fired in your company's (or your personal) direction. Shooters at both the corporate and individual level believe they are justified in firing upon targets because they have accepted their task based on perceived truths. Many shooters have solidly justifiable reasons for going after a target, even if the reason is only that the target exists on the other side of the shooter's perceived truth. Whether a real truth or a perceived truth, the shooter is going to use this information if it helps fulfill their task. Not everyone can become a Neo, and for those who aren't, there are a few things that can be learned to minimize exposure to these variable truths and, in turn, make dodging a bullet more possible. This is where the first element to "trust no one" comes into play. At minimum, adhere to the Ronald Reagan rule of "trust but verify."

Let's take a closer look at other techniques that can be used when dodging bullets.

CHAPTER 16

BEING AWARE AND PAYING ATTENTION

*Know your enemy and know yourself and you can
fight one hundred battles without disaster.*
—SUN TZU

wareness is such a critical tool when it comes to dodging bullets, and it sets the stage for shooting back when necessary. We've heard jokes on TV and radio about low-information people. This is usually used as a pejorative in the context of politics and world affairs, and is a name given to those people who do not or will not stay in tune with events taking place domestically and abroad. These people are ultimately the ones who complain about tax increases, changes in federal or state policies, crime, events that inconvenience them, and so on. They typically end their complaining with, "Well, I didn't know." They didn't know because they weren't paying attention. In the business world, from the CEO to the production worker, not being aware and not paying attention is what will get you figuratively killed.

With the wealth of information available to us today through the Internet, electronic news media, social media, cable TV, satellite radio, and even traditional print media, there is no excuse not to be informed. This holds particularly true when it comes to business. Given the number of cable news shows and business networks that are available, and the plethora of Internet sites one can visit, you would expect people to have at least a superficial interest in the events that can impact their lives. I never cease to be astounded by people who have never read their company website, never listened to or read the transcript from an earnings conference call, never visited client and supplier websites, failed to follow electronically activities of their leadership, or failed to track their company's overall financial performance. I have both heard and met individuals who have seen entire divisions in their company sold off or shut down and did not have the sense to make the connection regarding the potential impact to them. In some cases, they didn't even realize deals were being discussed. This is simply inexcusable, and the potential for these people to dodge a bullet is almost nonexistent.

Maybe another piece of dialogue that should have appeared in the *Matrix* example but didn't is the question: "When did you know that you no longer had to dodge bullets?" The answer should be: "When I became aware." If you're a CEO, you'd better know your business, your customers' businesses, and your suppliers' businesses better than your own board and better than the management of those related businesses. If you're an employee at any level, know your company and know your management. Watch them, observe them, and listen to what they say and don't say. Be astute enough to know that it's as important to know the market you sell to as it is to know the products you sell. Never let yourself be blindsided. It's very easy to pick off targets who are strangers to their own environment.

> *If you're not confused, you're not paying attention.*
> —TOM PETERS

One who is truly aware of her company and its markets will rarely be caught off guard. In a perfect world, she will never have to dodge a bullet, and she will never have to shoot back. Being aware allows you to see the guns before they are in the shooter's hands, and prepares you for a perfect dodge while setting you up in a position to be able to shoot back if and when necessary.

This rule applies equally for corporations and their leaders. Decisions are constantly being made at the political and social level that have serious ramifications and consequences for business. The practices of corporate manipulation and crony capitalism that exist in politics today are unlike anything we've ever seen. Corporate leadership that fails to be aware and stay ahead of the political maneuvering that is taking place may find their companies coming up short. Politicians today are trying to pick the winners and losers when it comes to technology, banking, health care, and other key industries. Politicians are very adept when it comes to understand the role of dodging bullets and shooting back, and they will draw from a broad range of shooters to accomplish their end game. Corporate executives must be in touch with all pending legislation that can potentially impact their business and, in fact, must stay ahead of the vultures who would seek to change their way of doing business.

Being aware and paying attention may be the most important advice this book has to offer because you can't dodge bullets and shoot back without it.

CHAPTER 17

Deflection

> *Men seek for vocabularies that are reflections of reality.*
> *To this end, they must develop vocabularies that are*
> *selections of reality. And any selection of reality must, in*
> *certain circumstances, function as a deflection of reality.*
> —*Kenneth Burke*

Most politicians are masters of deflection, and they use this technique to effectively defeat their rivals and to stay in office. We've seen them on the news responding to questions they were never asked and not answering the questions they were asked. Deflection is an excellent tool to be used when dodging bullets, but in business you have to be far more clever than politicians. Politicians are typically challenged by a media that, although capable of bringing them down, does not have the ability to terminate them. As a result, politicians can easily choose to deflect when challenged with uncomfortable questions or queries. Corporate situations don't lend themselves to the same type of deflection. Shooters in particular have a mission, and so by the time they have the gun in their hands, the ability to deflect becomes a far greater challenge. They ask a question, get the wrong answer, and *zap*, the buzzer goes off and another victim is dragged away.

Whenever possible, deflection needs to be initiated not only before the gun is in the shooter's hand but before the shooter even becomes a shooter. Deflection is not the tool of stupid people. Deflection is truly a rhetorical art form, and when mastered, it is quite impressive. Politicians may at times use deflection carelessly, but people in corporate situations don't have that luxury. In business, deflection needs to be part of a greater strategy. It is but one tool in the tool box and is really meant to parry a strike and then set up a counter-strike. In addition to being a tool for dodging bullets, deflection is also a tool that can be used to eventually position one for shooting back.

Just as words can be an effective tool in shooting bullets, they can be used equally as well in dodging them. This is particularly true when we look how they're used as a tool of deflection. One of my favorite words in the art of deflection is "although." "Although" is a word mastered by politicians and most savvy executives of public companies who have to do quarterly earnings calls. The use of this word allows the responder to take the dialogue in any direction they want, totally avoiding the question that was actually asked.

> **Analyst:** Mr. _____, it would appear that given current market conditions and with your revenues during the current quarter, that the prognosis for the coming quarters will not be good.
>
> **CEO:** Although there are some who think the current market conditions could impact our coming quarter earnings, let me tell you what I think about what's going on in the market.

Naturally, the executive goes on to redefine the market as he sees it and dismisses any suggestions that his future earnings will be impacted. It's not uncommon with executives to deflect difficult questions or comments onto their competitors, their suppliers, the government, or some world event. The extreme case of this is the person who's asks a challenging question and completely dismisses the question and changes topic.

> **Reporter:** Mr. President, what do you think about the current situation with Russia?
>
> **President:** I'm glad you asked that because it makes me think about what's going on in our economy.

It is astonishing how often these deflections go unchallenged, and because they do, people, particularly in leadership roles use them quite a bit. Let's face it: when the bullets are traveling toward you, pulling out a deflecting shield isn't a bad idea.

Deflection takes on many forms: i.e., humor, accusation, sincerity, intellectual, physical, and many other. The form it takes is fully predicated on the situation and the individuals involved. Many deflections can go wrong if individuals are not proactive in assessing a situation and the people involved. A serious situation might warrant a serious deflection, but it could also call for a humorous deflection. Each form of deflection sets the stage for a follow-up event, and therefore, it must be used wisely.

Let's take a look at some examples of deflection and its usefulness as a tool when dodging bullets. To start, *humor* is a fantastic deflection tool because it mitigates tension in a stressful situation. It is a disarming tool but also a dangerous tool to use, because when used inappropriately it can send the wrong message and turn you into a bigger target. Making light of a question or responding with a level of humorous sarcasm can absolutely disengage some shooters. It can also anger others who feel the response was an attempt to insult. Using humor with people who have no sense of humor can be disaster, while others might laugh and say, "You know, I never looked at this situation that way, but it is pretty silly."

Creating an artificial crisis or reorganizing priorities is also a deflection tool. This is a bit of the old story of "If you think that's bad, you obviously haven't heard about this," which now prioritizes a different crisis. "Your division is underperforming," says an executive. He gets the reply: "That may be true, but think of it in the context of the other divisions" (or current marketplace, or the performance of the competition). The boat may be taking on water, but the guy in the other boat in the race has already sunk. Clever shooters may never fall for this tactic because they've heard all the excuses, but you'd be amazed at how many people fall for this kind of simple deflection.

Deflection is used to buy time by getting others to take a look at something totally different. It's like someone bringing up a war in the Middle East and the response is, "How about them Yankees". As silly as it sounds, this kind of thing is done every day, and everyone appears to do it. This kind of tool can cut both ways. The victim will use it to slow down the shooter, but in some instances, the shooter will use it prior to their readiness to take a shot. For example, say a company is going through turmoil, and one employee who is potentially at risk goes to another employee who he doesn't recognize as being a shooter. The at-risk employee asks the shooter something like: "Given the challenges my division has had over the past few quarters, do you think

I'm at risk?" The shooter immediately deflects the question by saying something like: "Hey, how does your wife like that new car you got her?" No matter who is using this type of deflection, it is just an effort to avoid the elephant in the room and talk about other things in order to buy time.

Think in your own career how many times you use deflection as a tool. What were the results? Have you ever had to use it because you were a target? Did you use it well, or did it worsen the problem? How will you use it in the future if you're a target, and how will you use it in the future if you're a shooter? Knowing the answers to these questions may help you hit your target if you're the shooter and just may save your corporate life if you're the target.

CHAPTER 18

ACCUSATIONS: THE BLAME GAME

I couldn't quite understand how an ordinary
man's good qualities could become crushing
accusations against a guilty man.
—ALBERT CAMUS

Making an accusation and pointing fingers are "dodging bullet" tools that are significantly different then the far softer tool of deflection. There are people who might ask, "Well, aren't accusations a shooter's tool or a means of shooting back?" The answer is no, because accusations for the most part don't have enough substance behind them to survive most scrutiny. Once a target has been isolated and fired upon, it becomes extremely challenging to make accusations stick, and most shooters perceive them as a means of buying time—which is, in fact, what they are designed to do. Accusations are most effective prior to the gun being in the shooter's hand, which is still a point whereby those who are about to do the shooting revisit their expectation relative to those who are chosen to be eliminated. Accusations will never take out a shooter but could potential redirect the firing order to other individuals who may already be on the target list or toward those who might remain in question.

There are two forms of accusations: the "throw shit against the wall and see if it sticks" accusations and the substantive accusations. The "shit against the wall" accusations are typically an act of desperation designed to dodge a bullet at the last possible second. They are also an act of malice, as the shit that's being thrown can very often be directed at the wrong target. Now, I am not saying that it is impossible for these types of actions to get traction and even do some damage, because the reality is that they can and they do. The evidence of this is irrefutable when we look at business and politics. Whether or not these accusations gain traction is sometimes based only on whether individuals desire them to be true. In contrast, there are those accusations that are built on substantive data. Although these accusations have a chance to gain momentum, their effectiveness is skewed by the fact that they are being made by someone who not only has a target on his or her back but has already been shot at. Because the target waited so long to initiate the action, it fails to serve as a shooting-back tool and only exists as a dodging-bullet technique to once again buy the target some time.

Interestingly, accusations can play out at both the individual and the corporate level. How often have we seen scenarios where one corporation (the shooter) is making a hostile move on another company (the target)? The target may be running out of options to defend himself, so he resorts to accusing the acquiring company of being "bad guys." The targeted company may be buying time to bring in a more desirable acquirer or might wish to gain time to restructure and ward off any hostile attempts, so in order to accomplish this it begins hurling a multitude of accusations at the perceived hostile party. The targeted party might reach out to the media with a mudslinger's list of evil deeds on the part of the acquiring company. This is anything but a shooting-back maneuver, but it could be all the targeted company can do to stall the process and secure a stronger negotiating position. When this happens, the outcome never results in a win/win but usually does irreparable harm to both companies. Even if a deal is finally negotiated, the level of ill will that exists in the aftermath is enough to leave the new entity in a dysfunctional state for a long time.

When accusations are enlisted at the individual level to dodge a bullet, there are two possible motivations behind them. The low-information target will make accusations at more of an emotional level. This person naively believes that by redirecting a shooter's focus she can dodge a bullet and possibly save herself. There is always a chance she might gain a short reprieve while her company sorts through the accusations, but eventually the shooter will bring her down, and though she's dodged a bullet in the short term, the fact is she's not utilized her time wisely, if not to shoot back than at least to find an escape route. In contrast, the more savvy individual—the one who has been monitoring the company for a period of time and could see the inevitability that was coming—may hurl very targeted accusations to inhibit the shooter's rush to make a shot and gain time for herself to determine whether to shoot back or get out of town.

The thing about accusations is, they're designed to penetrate quite deeply, and if directed at coworkers who are not part of the target selection process (but rather those individuals one has had relationships with), then those accusations may become something from which neither the accuser nor the accused can ever recover. The truth is that people will do just about anything when trying to save their own skin, and unfortunately at that point, everyone else becomes fair game.

CHAPTER 19

DOUBT AND UNCERTAINTY

Doubt is an uncomfortable condition,
but certainty is a ridiculous one.
—VOLTAIRE

C reating doubt and uncertainty is also an effective way of dodging bullets. It is much more civilized than hurling accusations and far more compelling as well. Hurl an accusation, and it may be construed as sour grapes or irrational disappointment. Create a shield of doubt and uncertainty, and you may be able to avoid a lethal shot.

Planning an event that results in significant change with individual personnel or with an entire company is not an exact science. Certainty will always yield to clarity, but clarity has gaps of its own, and those gaps leave the door open for creating doubt and uncertainty. The first rule in creating doubt and uncertainty is to understand the dynamic in which the individual or the company finds itself. This requires putting one's self or one's company in the position of those who will be doing the shooting. It once again comes back to asking the tough questions:

- What gain is there to the company by taking this action?
- What problem does taking this action solve, and what benefit does the company derive?
- Are the decisions being motivated as a result of personal gain or corporate gain?
- What, if any, are the monetary issues driving the company's actions?

- (This question is asked from the company vantage point as related to an individual): Does this individual have any value left for the company, and if not, why? Could this person serve the company in a different capacity?
- (In situations involving company against company action): How does our action against or with this company help drive down our costs, mitigate our risks, and increase our profits?

I have little doubt you can add to the list or craft a question more appropriate to your situation, but hopefully this list will help you get started should you find yourself being shot at.

Once these questions are satisfactorily answered, without any level of self-deception, then the stage is set for the creation of doubt and uncertainty. As we have made clear throughout this section of the book, the earlier a target can take these actions, the more opportunity there is for some level of success. As with all dodging-bullet actions (whether involving a company or an individual), it has to be understood what the desired outcome is prior to utilizing this methodology. Will it be protection from an onslaught of bullets? Is it basically to buy time? Is it being initiated to create further doubt and uncertainty about every action being taken? All good questions need to be to be considered. There are no easy answers I can provide given that what's being address is far too subjective.

If clarity has its gaps, then the best way to obfuscate the situation is once again by using a Socratic form of questioning designed to motivate the decision makers to revisit their decisions. I must be clear on the point that all the dodging-bullet techniques being described are only applicable when the party being shot at has not committed any acts that are legally or morally inappropriate for the workplace. If that is the case, then there is no reason whatsoever not to challenge the shooting parties with respect to their action. The idea here is to get the decision makers to the point of challenging their own decisions. Cast enough doubt and uncertainty prior to them shooting their weapons, and you may save both yourself and your company.

CHAPTER 20

BEING A CHAMELEON

> *We are chameleons, and our partialities and prejudice*
> *change place with an easy and blessed facility, and*
> *we are soon wanted to the change and happy in it.*
> —*MARK TWAIN*

Chameleons represent my least favorite and my most favorite characters when it comes to dodging bullets, because I totally understand why an individual would adopt these characteristics. In some instances, chameleons are nothing more than sycophants who have one objective only, and that is to save their own ass. They are anything but stupid, and they've learned to play the corporate game better than others. These types of chameleons, however, typically lack any level of integrity. They are often individuals who will become assassins or other forms of shooters because it serves their purpose of staying alive. They will take out anyone necessary in order to succeed. Some chameleons are so good at what they do that they can make others believe they are actually the shooter, as opposed to being a target, even though that's exactly what they are. They go out of their way to blend in with whoever they believe is making the decisions. Their hope is that the shooter looks right past them and moves on to others.

Here's where I contradict myself. There is nothing wrong with actually being a chameleon, but one should do it in a way that allows him to maintain his integrity and professionalism. Chameleons who are proactive, smart, and have foresight are exceptional people. Although survival is their primary purpose, their actions and behavior are designed to result in something positive for themselves, their peers, and their company. Chameleons with these characteristics are looking to see how they can take a dangerous environment and turn it into something positive. They ask tough questions of themselves before taking action, such as: "What's good about this? How can this have a positive impact on the company? What can I do to turn this into a positive situation for myself? How will others perceive these actions, and how will they react? What must I do to stay one step ahead of the downside possibilities?" By asking better and better questions, this type of chameleon adjusts to the changing environment and blends in. She influences those who could be shooters by demonstrating her worth to the changing environment and how her presence is a necessity for the organization moving forward. Of course, she cannot achieve this unless she is aware. To be this kind of chameleon requires a level of bravery, because the process of blending in also makes her visible within the environment she's chosen to operate in. Even the bravest chameleon, however, knows when it's time to run for cover.

CHAPTER 21

RUNNING FOR COVER

As I was running for cover I came to realize that the best protection I had was inside of me.
—*HARRY ROZAKIS*

In the middle of a gunfight, there is no shame in running for cover. Even the most agile of chameleons, let alone the average employee, knows that you don't step outside when the bullets are flying on the street. To let yourself get caught in the cross fire clearly means you're not paying attention. There are a number of different ways employees and executives can run for cover, but it is critical to know what kind of cover is available, how accessible it is to you, and how long that cover will protect you. If someone is coming after you with a shotgun, a small empty cardboard box is not going to protect you. Chameleons attempt to hide in plain sight, but when they can't, they find the most protective covering they can. Trying to stay one step ahead by being cognizant of your environment is critical to survival.

One of the most important things to keep in mind when running for cover involves understanding who is hunting you. You need to know where you fall on the shooter's priority list and whether it is the shooter making the decision or someone else. This will play a huge role in deciding what kind of cover to take and when to take it. For example, I have spoken with individuals who have succeeded in dodging a bullet by becoming invisible but not by being a chameleon. These people simply thoroughly and completely removed themselves from the environment where the war was taking place. I have witnessed individuals who have taken two- and three-week road trips both domestically and internationally under the guise of attending to important customer-related matters. This can prove to be a double-edged sword, and so it is incredibly important for the individual to understand just how big a target he is and how committed the organization is to removing him.

Comprehending why you are a target in the first place will also be critical when making this decision. In one case, an individual disappeared to Asia for three weeks, only to come back to his headquarters and learn he had survived and actually ended up being promoted. It turned out that, though his department was targeted, he was recognized as a stellar performer and there were those in senior management who admired his perseverance in continuing to "comfort" customers during a period of turmoil. In another instance, an individual used a similar technique, believing that she would be a survivor if she was not readily available to those who would remove her from her position. She also took an extended trip but failed to realize that her situation was such that even if she was the best employee in the company there was simply no further role for her. She returned to find herself without access to her building. She was ultimately escorted to her desk to pick up her personal items, which had already been packed.

Taking cover does not typically save anyone, but it buys you the time that, had you been fully aware, you wouldn't have needed to make better decisions. There are some people who take cover behind their customers, their suppliers, their fellow employees, and in some instances, even their family. When individuals haven't been proactive in seeking protection or preparing to go on the offense, they will often seek shelter behind these other individuals. Using one's family is typically a sympathy play and almost never effective. The woman who says, "I have five children, no husband, and a mortgage," and implies that the loss of her position would put her out on the street may draw some compassion, but it is highly unlikely she will dodge a bullet. There are others who have built an invaluable relationship between a company customer or supplier in the hopes that these individuals will speak up for them and provide a level of protection. In these situations, the final result is the customer or supplier telling the company: "I'm sorry to see you lost so-and-so." Using fellow employees as a shield is also not uncommon. I have seen subordinates who hold their superiors up for protection in hopes that they can take an action that will save the person, and I have witnessed other times when a colleague or superior has been used as a shield to take the hit. (How foolish of those people to let themselves be put in that situation.) None of this provides the cover one needs.

There are some who think running for cover means getting a lawyer; it doesn't, as having a lawyer sometimes makes you a bigger target than you already are. (This is something we'll address in more detail in the "shooting back" section of this book.) Others believe running for cover means seeking protection from a corporate or business ally. In small business and "Ma and Pop" shops, running for cover could mean finding solace from a family member or business founder. In large corporations, individuals sometimes run to the management of other divisions, seeking to secure a transfer ahead of their potential demise from a department, group, or division. The fact is, running for cover as I've described rarely works, and only on very unusual occasions does this ensure one's ability to dodge a bullet.

If you are going to have to run for cover, look within yourself. Other people and obstacles are not going to save you, and they are not going to hide you. The greatest source for finding cover is in your head. If you're going to be dodging bullets, you need to look for answers in a way that secures a positive outcome. If you haven't already established a plan of action, understand that intellectual cover may be the answer for finding a longer-term solution. One means of finding cover is to create intelligent questions that are applicable to whatever your current situation is. Force those who would take you out to think about their actions, and force them not to hurry their decisions by making them think and look for answers. Not all corporate executions (individual or group) are well thought out, no matter how hard decision makers attempt to make it appear that way. Tough questions create layers of resiliency and buy time. Don't think for a moment, however, that those layers will provide indefinite protection. Seeking protection using this methodology is truly a game of "cat and mouse," and only very smart mice get away unscathed.

CHAPTER 22

Insight and Experience

> *For those who are examined, instead of being*
> *angry with themselves, are angry with me!*
> —Socrates

D uring some of the most challenging times of my career, I have fallen back on Plato's *Apology* as a source of thought and steadfastness. *Apology* is said to be the speech Socrates gave while defending himself against accusations of corrupting the young. A snapshot of this goes as follows. When Socrates learns the Oracle at Delphi stated that there is no wiser man on earth than he, Socrates heartily disputes this and seeks out those who are wiser. Though he fails in the task, he still rejects the assertion that he is the wisest man alive and says there must be those who are wiser. As we have all learned, there is no shortage of people who are prepared to step up and offer advice, particularly when it comes to dodging bullets. Plato reminds us through Socrates's words that our own insight and experience may prove to be the most valuable tool we have.

> *Paladin: I sometimes think that all good men are afraid.*
> *It's also been said that fear is the beginning of wisdom.*
> —Have Gun—Will Travel, "Beau Geste,"
> Season 6, Episode 5 (1962)

Insight and experience make us wise, and it is wisdom that affirms for us there must be those who are wiser. To believe one is the wisest man in the room is an act of hubris, not wisdom. The attributes of insight and experience in themselves become the attributes necessary for dodging bullets. Insight and experience are not specific to age, race, gender, or anything else, and many of us have heard the expression of an individual being wise beyond his or her years. The majority of successful entrepreneurs are successful because of the failures and struggles they've experienced and don't want to experience again, even when their professional career has been short or limited. Nevertheless, they walk away with knowledge, which if used properly, will become demonstrable wisdom in the future.

Too often, those who are under fire make the mistake of assessing themselves, which is a wise thing to do. But more importantly, they should be assessing those who are shooting at them while surveying the environment in which those shots are taking place. If an individual has self-awareness and smarts, then she needs to spend her time focused on the real reason she is dodging bullets. Earlier in this book, we identified the types of shooters we can expect encounter in business; part of the reason for this was to teach those who might come under fire exactly how to assess and if possible avoid shooters. Very often those doing the shooting are not self-aware and are actually deflecting onto their coworkers. In a business, division, or group where leadership has failed, the failure of those in charge is often denied. Individuals who are under fire need to be cognizant of the fact that they may be under fire simply because of someone else's failures. This knowledge doesn't lessen the threat, but it does help in knowing just how to dodge a bullet.

Our friend Socrates teaches us that asking the right series of questions and comprehending the answers we get back goes a long way in determining who may be the wisest person in a conflict. We should, however, remember that as with Socrates, wisdom alone does not ensure your survival. Like many dodging-bullet techniques, the Socratic method buys you time when you need it the most.

CHAPTER 23

Dodging Bullets: Securing a Position

In the animal kingdom, one of the keys to survival
is to outwit your enemies. And when you're
surrounded by carnivores, one of the best strategies
is to fade into the background and disappear.
—Neil deGrasse Tyson

As we've already indicated, dodging bullets is not a long-term solution, but it is a necessity when engaged on the corporate battlefield. Even the most skilled bullet dodgers will ultimately be struck if all they do is spend their time dodging bullets. It should be clearly understood that if you've dodged a bullet, there is another one out there with your name on it. Sometimes it can take weeks and sometimes it can take years, but if someone has taken a shot at you once, in all likelihood you will be shot at again. Your task is to figure out how not to let that happen.

A crucial objective of dodging bullets comes down to securing a position that gives you time to plan and strategize. Never make the mistake of thinking that because you dodged one or two bullets, you are safe. The shooters are always out there, and they will come gunning for you again. This is why securing a position is so critical. Some of the techniques we've described thus far can buy some amount of time, but they are not indicative of *securing a position*. Securing a position involves putting yourself in a place where you can truly get as good a view as possible of the action taking place without being in the line of anyone's fire. Depending on the specific situation, it is a short-term solution for camouflaging the target on your back and providing a respite from the battleground. Finding a secure position is not easy and provides no guarantee of survival. The obvious question is, how does one secure a position? What does a position look like? Who would and should know about such a position? When do you actually leave a secure position?

Earlier we spoke about individuals who were successful in avoiding taking a bullet because they were traveling domestically or internationally "attempting to build the company's business." As we said, depending on your overall vulnerability, travel can buy you time. It may not protect you, but it can provide the few extra days you might need to determine your next actions. I have seen countless examples of this throughout my career. Sometimes it has been absolutely humorous to see how an individual has outfoxed those gunning for him. As an executive, I have also seen enough of these examples to ensure that these techniques have not been used against me or the company I operate.

Let's look at one example of using the travel strategy to secure a position. Imagine an individual who is traveling overseas or domestically (overseas typically provides greater cover) and knows about or anticipates that the current turmoil in the company will directly impact her survival in the organization. This person immediately realizes that the balance of her travel can be utilized to set a strategy that might include taking countermeasures while traveling, setting up the stage for shooting back, or possibly coordinating an exit. In this scenario, the individual is shrewd enough to take advantage of her time to substantiate her risk. Once the risk is confirmed, she begins lining up possible career opportunities outside her company. She ensures all her key contacts are made aware that there could be a change approaching and their assistance might be needed. If she believes her impending demise might require legal countermeasures, she puts them in place prior to her return.

I recall one individual who, having learned that a major restructuring occurred while he was traveling, positioned himself to return on a weekend. Fully aware that there was a chance of encountering a shooter or at least the HR department upon arrival at work Monday morning, he decided to access headquarters over the weekend and clean out all his personal affects and critical files. He also took advantage of the time out of town to contact his attorney and set up job interviews, which ultimately secured him a position within two weeks of leaving his company. The key point here is, he bought the necessary time under the cover of traveling.

Travel is not always an option for some individuals, but fortunately there are often secure locations in plain sight. The duration and the degree of the security of these locations are dependent on each situation and how widespread the impact is in the company. There is a distinct difference between one individual who has been targeted versus situations that affect an entire division or company. In a one-on-one situation, it is extremely difficult to find any sanctuary once you've been targeted. This is why knowing the shooters in advance can protect you. In a war games scenario or even a drone strike, the opportunity exists to step aside for a given period of time if one is paying attention. I have witnessed individuals who have been totally cognizant of their impending demise and have gained highly valued additional time by initiating things like making sure they are enrolled in an off-site training course, establishing relationships with people who can run short- or long-term interference for them, making sure they used their vacation time during the most critical period, and/or finding refuge by setting up and managing a critical customer, supplier, or financial meeting. If you're the executive who is justified in removing an individual or individuals, you need to become sensitized to just how creative people can be when their professional life is challenged. If you're the one whose life is being challenged, you'd better think of every technique and excuse possible for finding and maintaining a secure position.

Chameleons are very good at finding secure positions because of their ability to blend into a changing or disruptive situation. They are capable for a period of time of making it appear as though they have joined the side in charge, and by doing so, they can prepare themselves, planning their next steps. Smart chameleons recognize that their ability to turn colors only lasts for a limited period of time, and as a result, they disappear as quickly as they appear. When they move, they move quickly, and then just as quickly they change their color again.

CEOs and presidents of companies are usually better off than subordinates within a company when it comes to finding a secure position—first and foremost because they are privy to more information than others in the company. This is not to say that top executives can't be blindsided by their board members or shareholders, but in the majority of situations, the top executive has a good sense when something negative is about to come down. I am aware of some CEOs who are so good at what they do that they actually turn things around so that their board comes under fire. Most CEOs recognize that departure or removal are the inevitabilities that come with the job, and because of that, they make preparations well in advance of any event. Understanding the insecure nature of their position actually puts them in a secure position to plan and do what they need to. However, the fact is that all employees can be as prepared as the CEO when it comes to finding a secure position if they are willing to believe that whatever their position in the company, they will never be secure. The days of those who live and work for the same company for thirty years and are handed a watch and in some cases a pension are becoming more and more rare. You end up only being as secure as your last paycheck, and yet the same employers who insist on loyalty know they can remove you in an instances and even on a whim. As a result, all employment must be regarded as being discretionary. This is why the best time for dodging bullets is before the gun is in the shooter's hand.

When you secure a position, this enables you to determine whether you are in a position to be shooting back or, for that matter, if you even want to shoot back. Taking a secure position enables you to think more clearly and be proactive as opposed to reactive. The secure position hopefully buys you enough time to determine if shooting back should be an option, whether you should continue to dodge bullets for a while longer, or if you should find a way to extricate yourself from the situation completely. If you choose to shoot back, a secure position can give you the necessary prep time, because shooting back is not easy.

SECTION III

Shooting Back

> *In any game, you have an enemy coming at yourself that you have to shoot. If you go back to "Space Invaders," they shoot at you when they come at you, so how are you going to protect yourself? You're going to shoot, and that is a typical videogame.*
> —*Hideo Kojima*

CHAPTER 24

A PURPOSE-DRIVEN EFFORT

*A clear purpose not only defines what we
do, it defines what we don't do*
—*RICK WARREN*, THE PURPOSE DRIVEN CHURCH

Shooting back is not easy, and it can sometimes get you killed. To be successful at shooting back, you must learn or know how to shoot. This means planning and then planning some more. It will require questioning every action you are about to make prior to initiating. Successfully shooting back will demand that you execute with the precision of a marksman. Execution and the resulting success is what it comes down to ultimately. The key here involves defining success. Engaging in an ongoing gun battle is very doable, but where does that leave you (unless your intent is to just make the other side miserable)?

Everyone who engages in shooting back has different parameters when it comes to defining success. For some, it's a matter of personal pride and proving they were right. There are others who seek redemption and possibly even reinstatement. Still others are just looking for peace of mind. Then there are those looking for payback. So let's get serious for a moment. If an individual begins shooting back in a business environment, it should be for no other reason than monetary reward and enrichment. Anything else is artificial and short-lived, because all the things you believed were righteous and all the wrongs you believe you can fire back on are nothing more than history. So if you're not in it for a monetary result, don't waste your precious time shooting back—move on!

The concept of shooting back creates an interesting juxtaposition, because the target becomes the shooter and the shooter becomes the target. There is a *High Noon*–like quality to this when the field is leveled, which it rarely is. When this does occur, it is not always the fastest person to the draw who wins. In most instances, it is the individual who is better prepared and better armed. Shooting back must *never, never, never* be emotional if you hope to survive. The "they shot Charlie, so I'm gonna shoot them scenario" is doomed from the start, and there is certainly no monetary reward attached. Like the guy who runs out to save Charlie, emotion is nothing more than you crying out "shoot me"—and that's exactly what will happen. In business, shooting back is a calculated risk and the stakes are very high. Besides losing one's job or career, one might go broke and one might never work again at the level he was at. Shooting back will destabilize your life for a while and possibly forever. Individuals—and organizations, for that matter—who find themselves in a shooting-back position need to accept from the outset that they are in a reactive position, and they must find a methodology for turning the tide and ending up in a proactive role. That means hitting back harder and with greater force than the initial shooting party or, alternatively, being evasive and deceptive enough to hit the original shooting party before they even realized there would be a counterattack.

Like any other battle, when you make the choice to shoot back using overpowering weapons, you need to ensure the weapons you are choosing are as overpowering as you believe them to be and you need to select weapons appropriate for the battle in which you are about to engage. This is a point that is important to grasp. What might be used in a battle with a large corporation might be exactly the wrong tool to use in a small company or "Ma and Pop shop"-type battle. Remember, bullets come from all different directions. Though we commonly think of a superior terminating a subordinate, we can realize an entirely different scenario if a group of subordinates or a labor pool is taking shots at individual management or the entire corporate hierarchy.

One reality that is sometimes rejected by those shooting back is the role of money. Understanding the monetary component (how it works and how to use it) significantly influences the success component, which is also money. Money pays for your weapons in most cases, and money becomes the motivation behind the weapons you amass and your opponent amasses. Outside of possibly wanting to punch someone in the nose, the initial response of someone who has been shot and now wishes to shoot back is: "I'll get a law-yer." And well you might. If you manage to appoint an attorney, realize that he supports your position for one purpose only: so he can be paid. Even in whis-tleblower situations where attorneys agree to operate on contingency, their loyalty to their client and their commitment to the cause is directly linked to a monetary outcome. Attorneys are never the shooters; they are the weapon of shooters. They can only fire with the ammunition they're given, and they can only hit the targets their client aims them at.

So let's examine the kind of ammunition that can be loaded in your weap-on, and let's determine who and how to select the target. Whether you're a cor-poration or an individual firing back, data is a huge factor in your arsenal of ammunition. Data provides a trail, a history, and a means for casting doubt on an action that's been taken. Data can be the gunpowder that determines the amount of damage that can be done when striking the target. People—mean-ing coworkers, peers, management, friends, and family—are also tools in one's arsenal. The issue with people is one of reliability. You can't fire back if you have a weapon with a high risk of misfiring. Coworkers, professional peers, and management acquaintances with links to the business are not always reli-able when shooting back. Those who work for the company will always be restrained in their defense of you due to the monetary component. As an old Chinese saying goes, "Loyalty belongs with those who fill your rice bowl." So unless you're in a position to improve an individual's life in real dollars or a monetary equivalent, expect these weapons to misfire. Some have even been known to blow up in your hand. The scenario is much the same as "friendly fire." Invariably there will be that individual who feels that sharing your in-tention to shoot back with those who are already shooting at you will help improve the situation and reinstate the order of things. Really?

Family and friends not associated with the business in any capacity can be reliable to a point but are rarely a high-impact weapon. Their strength can increase if the situation ends up in a courtroom and when some kind of physi-cal or psychological damage has been caused, but the reality is, the chance of a shooting-back scenario ending up in court is highly limited. Where friends and family can be vital to your shooting back relates to the emotional reload-ing that will need to take place. As we've said, shooting back can, depending on the severity of the situation and your desired outcome, be highly destruc-tive if not managed. Part of that management is the support one receives from friends and family. When these battles last a long time, those around you begin to wear out and can cease providing the support you require. This is why it's important to educate them as best you can about the challenges of shooting back.

Where the friends-and-family situation becomes complex is when the battle wages within a family- or friend-owned business. Evidence of this has been displayed in families with powerful names like Rockefeller, Du Pont, and Morgan, as well as in small family businesses. I have personally spoken with and witnessed small family businesses that have been torn apart because of shooting-back scenarios. A family member proposes a change in the business or possibly the sale of the business, and then that family member is asked to leave the business. A battle ensues, and before you know it you have a highly polarized family at war with one another. When this scenario ends positively, it is normally in the form of compromise, but when it ends up badly, this typically involves the destruction of the business and possibly the breakdown of the entire family. As we said earlier, if there is no monetary reward, then what's the point of shooting back? Because shooting back can sometimes involve no more than negotiating the financially best separation possible for you. Lastly, never, ever pick up a gun unless you intend to use it.

CHAPTER 25

WHEN THE MEDIA BECOMES YOUR POSSE

When the media becomes your posse, your chances
of winning the battle escalate considerably.
—*HARRY ROZAKIS*

Another weapon used in shooting back is the media. Depending on the scope of the situation, this could be the news media, social media, or the town crier (there once really was such a person). If the injustices stated in a story are compelling enough and the size and scope is something that could spark interest within a large local or national audience, then the news media can definitely prove to be a shooting-back tool. Whistleblowers have effectively used news outlets to get their story out. The television and print media can accomplish anything, from embarrassing a company to bringing a company to its knees, depending on the severity of the situation. Cigarette cases, drug cases, oil spills, and vehicle crashes are all instances where individuals who have been punished by their employer for confronting management with a potentially hazardous situation have been punished by their company and struck back via the media. Unfortunately, some media outlets don't vet the story as well as they should and end up punishing the wrong parties or those who have the greatest public profile. Anyone considering using traditional news media outlets for shooting back needs to realize that these vehicles will be very discerning in terms of what stories they choose to pick up. Just like with lawyers, the driver for the news outlet is viewership or readership, which will drive greater revenues. Although the intent behind going to traditional media might be noble, there will always be the underlying tone of a settlement.

Social media has provided an entirely new forum for shooting back, but it is also a two-way street in that if you're prepared to dish out dirt on this digital medium, you'd best be prepared to receive it. Social media has become the new Wild, Wild West when it comes to shooting back. Typically, individuals or organizations using social media as a vehicle to gain satisfaction or redemption are motivated by emotion and rarely get the satisfaction of a monetary reward. Social media is really nothing more than a harassment tool in the scheme of shooting back. That is not to say that harassment doesn't get results, because it does. The "squeaky hinge does get the grease," or in this instance, the cash. Rightfully or wrongfully, most companies want to settle these disputes in order to move forward. Those who post emotionally will rarely see a settlement, because their language is typically harsh and their threats often idle. Smart companies wait these individuals out because they end up boring people and ultimately the story goes away. What is most dangerous to a corporation is an individual who manipulates social media intelligently by posting factual and in some case irrefutable information. Many companies today have individuals who directly monitor social media sites to ensure no ill will is directed their way.

When the media becomes your posse, your chances of winning the battle escalate considerably. If you follow this path, you need to realize there is a time limit for achieving your end game. The media (whether print or social) tends to get caught up in the moment and has very little staying power. They are capricious and impatient for quick results so they can demonstrate their power. In addition, they can turn on you if the battle is not won quickly.

CHAPTER 26

The Good, the Bad, and the Ugly

If your culture is not well defined and if your leaders do not embody it, you will find that it falls to the lowest common denominator. Employees will begin to see where expectations are set based on those around them and will sink to that level. You'll find that you've become The Bad or even worse, The Ugly.
—Robert Swisher, CTO, "The Good, the Bad, and the Ugly: Who's on Your Team?" Business. com Media Inc. (April 10, 2014)

Shooting back is also a matter of who you are shooting back against. There are good corporations, and there are bad and ugly corporations. Good corporations know that when they go through major schisms in their business (such as mass layoffs or the removal of a high-profile individual from their company), there are going to be repercussions. Good companies are typically dealing with events where the company or its leadership has confronted a situation where key decisions have to be made. Very often those decisions will hurt people both personally and financially. The actions are normally undertaken to save the organization by effecting a critical change. Good corporations know there will be negative "blow back," so they take a proactive and pragmatic approach. They realize quite readily that a pat on the back along with a reasonable check go a long way toward easing tensions. Although it may cost them more upfront, it protects them from having a mob shooting back at them.

When shooting back at a good corporation, one needs to set realistic expectations as to what the maximum payout will be. Good companies will put forth what appear to be very generous separation agreements. This is, of course, intended to mitigate the amount of shooting back that takes place. There is always an attempt in these instances to do what's "fair" as they interpret fair. When dealing with a group, the company will socialize the issue, but when it involves an individual, the company will make the effort to explain the fairness of its offer in hopes that the person appreciates the company's effort. When one is shooting back, one should never accept the socialization of a group as a rebuttal, nor should she accept the old adage that the company has benchmarked the settlement against others in the industry or, in many cases, an employment contract. Both are meaningless. Dealing with a good company means being smart when you shoot back but also being rational in your "ask." All settlements come with upper limits, so your job is to ferret out what those upper limits are and ensure you max out. You do this by asking smart questions and building a strong argument. There is little risk in turning down first offers. Smart companies for the most part recognize smart people and treat them with respect.

Bad and ugly companies are an entirely different story and are much more difficult to deal with when it comes to shooting back. Bad companies typically have leadership that suffers from severe hubris and is unable to see its role in the events that led to the firing of an individual or group of individuals. Companies who follow the "bad or ugly" model are normally belligerent and use threats and other punitive actions to intimidate those who imply they might shoot back. Companies that attempt to break contracts with employees in order to effect change and minimize exposure are ugly companies. If amending contracts is something that could be necessitated, then it should have been done well in advance of a crisis. Bad and ugly companies believe stories of their own invulnerability because they see themselves as having layers of protection, both monetary and legal. The key to shooting back at bad and ugly companies is to simply not be as dumb or as evil as they are.

I came across a story of a CEO who had taken a public company through very turbulent times. Although she had turned the company around, in doing so she had challenged members of her board, some who ceased to be enamored with her once positive results were achieved. Very early on, the CEO was aware of the warning shots being fired her way. So to avoid ending up in a contentious situation, the CEO, who was under contract, volunteered to have her contract settled and voluntarily leave the company. Instead of coming to a reasonable agreement, the more belligerent board members did not want to settle since the CEO's contract would be in force and a fairly large payout would have to be made. Not being pragmatic, some members of the company's board attempted to use intimidation tactics to get the CEO to resign of her own accord but without honoring her contract. When the CEO declined, the hostility increased by those board members who were now incensed with the fact that they were not going to easily get their way. Unfortunately, these individuals had enough of a majority to override the cooler heads on the board. The fact that the board had become so emotionally tied to this issue created an ideal shooting-back situation for the CEO, who never became emotional or vindictive during the process. The board threatened the CEO that if she did not agree to waive her contract, it would put out a press release telling the world she had been fired. Anticipating these types of tactics, the CEO already had her shooting-back plans in place. The board followed through with its threat, and the CEO was removed. Given this was a public company, what the emotional board members failed to remember was that the CEO was a member of the board and based on the bylaws could not simply be terminated from her board seat. By moving forward with some very well-planned and executed actions, including the threat of showing up at both a board meeting and a shareholders meeting, the CEO was able to finally get the smarter individuals on the board to prevail and agree to settle the executive package. What the more hostile board members thought would prove to be an embarrassment for the CEO turned out to be an embarrassment for the company—which in actuality, the company was never able to recover from.

Success when shooting back means never losing sight of the monetary outcome. There are two sides to this, however. For example, if you're a company that's been fired upon, this is normally because there is some organization or individual out there who is trying to secure either cash or something that can be monetized. Success for a corporation when shooting back may not be direct monetary gain but rather a mitigation of a settlement they might have to make. Drug companies very often find themselves in the cross hairs of government agencies or ambulance-chasing attorneys who are seeking settlement dollars. Now, I am not writing to take a position on the side of all big pharmaceutical companies, and I will certainly not minimize the loss of life by an individual who takes a drug that is supposed to help him or her, but the reality of life is that these things happen. A drug that saves hundreds of thousands of lives and cost billions of dollars to develop but is taken by one or a handful of individuals who react badly to it or die is more than a little tragic, and there should absolutely be a level of compensation for the aggrieved. It is, however, tragic when there is an attempt to destroy financially that same company that has saved thousands of lives and crush its ability to continue research going forward. The fact is, life is filled with risk, whether it's eating a food product, driving a car, swimming in the ocean, or getting on a ride in an amusement park. When negligence is involved, there must absolutely be a level of compensation, but that is the rub, because in some instances there is a gray area between perceived carelessness and an act of fate. In the case of the pharmaceutical company, it is shooting back to protect itself from annihilation to continue to save lives going forward. Hopefully, it can walk away from the fight with a flesh wound. That is the measurement of success.

One of the final scenes in the movie *The Good, the Bad, and the Ugly* gets played out all the time in business, whether at the individual or corporate level. Ugly companies and individuals always end up with either no bullets in their gun or no gun in their holster and thus no gain from the gunfight. The "bad" typically and hopefully lay where they once stood, and the "good" ride off into the sunset with their bags of gold. So when you find yourself in a gunfight, which part do you want to play?

CHAPTER 27

THE NUCLEAR OPTION: "THE LAST GREAT ACT OF DEFIANCE!"

All good work is done in defiance of management.
—BOB WOODWARD

The nuclear option is clearly the last great act of defiance in the various manifestations of shooting back. It is a means of fighting back that can be used by individuals and companies alike, although the likelihood of this occurring with large or publicly traded companies is very slim given the plethora of laws and regulations in place to protect shareholders against the emotional or misguided behavior of corporate leaders. Ironically and naively, there are parties who engage in this option with the false belief that it will result in their winning, when in fact it will result in the ultimate loss; mutually assured destruction. Far more dangerous under the nuclear option are those individuals or companies who understand completely the ramifications of their actions and yet proceed to execute. It may be hard to fathom that any company or any sensible-thinking individual(s) would be willing to sacrifice their own career and reputation to bring down another party, but who says everyone in business is sensible?

The nuclear option can be illustrated in cases of employee versus company, company versus employee, and company versus company. Of the three, the employee versus company scenario is probably the most comprehendible because in 99 percent of the cases it can be driven by emotion. In its most dangerous form it occurs when you have a presumed rational individual or group of individuals who knowingly and methodically plan on utilizing this strategy, as they are far less likely to make a mistake than those who operate purely on emotion.

Emotional individuals are fundamentally looking for "payback" and for the party that has wronged them to suffer the way they have suffered as a result of a termination, dismissal, or layoff. Interestingly, this does not discriminate based on the rank the individual(s) held in the company prior to termination. Those people who were unable to dodge a bullet during a corporate showdown quite often have enough life left in them to fire back with a vengeance, and the nuclear option is the ultimate when it comes to firing back. If you are the executive of a company, it can prove extremely dangerous if you casually dismiss the ability of an individual to effectively use the nuclear option against a corporation. The "mouse that roared" is a great deal more than just an expression or a movie. An individual or group hell-bent on payback will use all available tools. It should be understood that the nuclear option, as employed by an individual or group challenging a company, by our definition only encompasses those things that are legally and morally acceptable. Retribution of a criminal nature is exactly that—criminal—and should be dealt with swiftly through the appropriate legal channels.

Understanding the emotional motivations of people is by no means a reason to ignore their actions and behavior. The fact that they are unconcerned about what happens to themselves means they're unconcerned about the outcome for others. If ever there was a situation where collateral damage might occur, this is one of them. These people typically believe their career has come to an end and, whether true or not, see the future as very bleak. Emotional individuals will typically use harassment as the first weapon of choice. Harassment may take on a multitude of forms operating in parallel. Making contact with the company's customers, suppliers, board of directors, and others affiliated with the business may all be avenues of pursuit by those who feel victimized. The emotional individual will call existing and past employees: those offering a sympathetic ear, as well as those they know they can rile up. If it is a group that feels victimized, their outreach may be significantly greater. This can lead to real traction, particularly if a business or shop is organized. There should be a full expectation that this type of individual(s) will engage with attorneys, contact the media if the story is credible, and seek every vehicle possible for disparaging the company's reputation and detracting from its brand. They can protest individually or as a group within the community outside the workplace, and as we've seen on the news, there are occasions where the individual or group shows up at the homes of executives. This borders on criminal and mob action, and again should be immediately be redirected to the authorities. Obviously, the bigger and more high profile the company, the greater the exposure. The "I don't care what happens to me in the end" attitude by a group or individual can be more lethal to a business than most businesses anticipate.

Companies will take shots at some individuals expecting that they understand the business dynamic that resulted in them being taken out, and as a consequence, the company mistakenly assumes the employees will leave quietly. They assume that because there is no emotional response by those being shot, the situation has stabilized itself. The nonemotional target may not be as vitriolic as the emotional target, but this does not mean they are less vindictive. The nonemotional people who choose the nuclear option are calculating and normally very, very smart. Though possibly harboring some deep-seated emotion, their focus is to get on with the business at hand (payback) regardless of what transpires next. These individual will employ and deploy the same weapons as the more emotional individual, but the planning behind their actions provides the opportunity to deliver a far more destructive blow. Their approach will be more thoughtful and methodical. They see time as their friend, so whether they act sequentially or in parallel is of no consequence to them. The objective is simple: bring down the company or those behind the company who took a shot at them and inflicted pain. Many of the people these individuals enlist to support their effort will give that support because they see an element of nobility in the battle they are undertaking. This is based on the idea that someone who would be willing to sacrifice everything must have truth and honor on their side, and therefore, if necessary the people around them will participate in the individual's martyrdom.

Think about whistleblowers. There are many very noble and honorable people who have fought against the odds in taking on a company where they have seen injustices, bad behavior, and actual violations of the law by company leadership. These people when successful appear on 60 Minutes, Dateline, and other so-called news shows. They have rightfully claimed their fifteen minutes of fame, and they have served the majority of us by bringing to light a situation that might harm the greater good. These people take on the battle, understanding that the outcome for them may not be positive. If you are a group or an individual who winds up in such a situation, pursuing the nuclear option may in fact be your only option. What happens, however, when an individual who has been removed from a business is not so noble but rather just vindictive? There is not a company in the world that doesn't have elements of misdoings in its history, decisions that were made, not maliciously or for corporate gain, but were simply the wrong choices by human beings in a business environment of changing dynamics. These decisions, when known to certain individuals, can be exploited when those individuals are suddenly put in a situation of shooting back. The reality is that not all whistleblowers, nor those people who are shooting back, are necessarily right. Companies and management teams are not always bad guys, and those they've engaged shooters to remove may be justifiable targets. The problem is, it is very difficult to battle those who are hell-bent on destruction to the point of sacrificing themselves.

Companies that use the nuclear option when going after an individual or group for the most part do so without realizing that the actions they're engaged in have nuclear ramifications. Hubris, ego, and invulnerability can all be part of the collective makeup of a company, whether big or small, publicly traded or "ma and pop" owned. There are those who allow themselves to believe that by enlisting shooters and removing individuals, groups, divisions, and partners, they are acting on behalf of the greater good, and thus they provide self-justification for these actions. If the individual has taken a shot at the company first, then their actions only gain greater validation. There are companies and management teams that truly believe being indifferent at best and coldhearted at worst is the best means for removing problems. These companies don't see these types of actions as being nuclear because they somehow convince themselves they are in the right and that their actions are thus acceptable. The issue here is, those who have just had a nuclear warhead dropped on them intend to retaliate, and that retaliation will be with as much force as is necessary, because in reality they perceive themselves as having nothing to lose. Companies should never assume that because they are capable of launching nuclear that the little guy is not capable of retaliating in kind.

So how and why does a company launch a nuclear strike on an individual? As already cited, some companies operate on a level of arrogance and hubris to the degree where they don't recognize that their launch of a nuclear action could potentially ensure their own destruction. There is a mentality here that the resources of the company are so great that no one individual or small group of people would ever be able to withstand the assault the company can level on them. We see this quite often with misguided boards that are ousting their CEO or management team. The assumption is that they are too big to be harmed by any retaliation and probably are big enough to withstand anything that is hurled in their direction. There is an element of truth to this when we are addressing large publicly traded companies, though there are numerous instances of corporate battles becoming public to the point where the shareholders have ultimately taken the hit. The large corporation may survive, but the result may be that not only was the management team ousted but so was the board that initiated that ousting.

Smaller companies, privately owned companies, and "Ma and Pop" shops can suffer from the same false pride that larger corporations do, and so they may choose to use a nuclear option against an employee(s) as a form of retribution or personal hostility. We have seen this in companies where an employee attempts to shake up a company and challenge management decisions—very much like the example we gave in the "Gunsmoke" chapter. In smaller businesses, personalities come into play at a much higher level, and the actions taken by both parties are based on historical situations and emotional decision making. With smaller companies, going nuclear doesn't typically work out well, particularly if you're going after those who are likely to retaliate. Yes, there are those who will be intimidated, but as a company, is this a gamble you're willing to take? Do you really want to try and predict which employees will go nuclear when shooting back and those who will not? I would hope not, because a former employee, even if he only has an impact on one client or one existing employee, might just have enough to seriously impact the business. Plus, what in actuality is there to be gained?

There is no need for any company to pursue the nuclear option with an individual, particularly for small companies. To do so is not only careless, it is stupid. At the beginning of this section, we indicated that the validity in shooting back is calculable to how much money is gained by the shooting party. There are, as we've already discussed, individuals and at times companies deploying nuclear options. Given that this option is for the most part a no-win scenario, what should be done to thwart it if you're a business? This is where that dirty word "accommodation" comes into play. Those individual who decide to shoot back by going nuclear on a company know they are never getting their position back, and that is part of the reason they decided to go nuclear in the first place. Companies finding themselves in this situation need to find paths toward de-escalation and if need be do so through accommodations. In these instances, cash may not be enough of a motivation because you're dealing with an individual whose motivations are linked to personal pride. If the individual does not expect to get her job back, then you need to ask yourself what it is that they want. There is not an easy answer to this, given that every individual and every situation is different. The job of a good human resources team and of good management is to determine what this person wants and what level of accommodation will be granted. Will it work in every instance? Absolutely not. But it is a better option than the one sitting on the table.

CHAPTER 28

THE STANDOFF: STALEMATE

Like the eye of a hurricane, the silence
of a standoff is deafening.
—*HARRY ROZAKIS*

As we have affirmed a number of times, shooting back does not always ensure victory. Nevertheless, it is certainly a way to create a serious cause for concern for those who have been shooting at you and set them scrambling for options of their own. Whether a company or an individual, shooting back makes the other side realize that whatever actions are in play (whether it be the takeover of the company or the elimination of your job)…the message is very clear to those who took the first shot that they are now in a gunfight.

There was a time when those being shot at had little recourse, simply because the rules weren't designed to help the underdog and the costs were beyond most individuals' capabilities. I should pause for a moment and make clear here that even big corporations can be the underdog when government, media, labor groups, and others set their sights on them. Fortunately or unfortunately, the proliferation of protective legislation and law firms has aided underdogs in their efforts to shoot back. I say "unfortunately" because in a number of instances a regulatory environment established to allegedly assist individuals and corporations has also been abused by government agencies seeking to fire their own shots. The other problem with so-called protective legislation is that is all too often written in ambivalent terms. One only need look at Sarbanes-Oxley for a firsthand example.

The manipulation of the media (social, print, television), as suggested earlier, has contributed to the arsenal one can build when shooting back. The point is that there are a variety of weapons available to those doing the shooting, just as there are for those shooting back. Given that these weapons are available to the shooter and those being shot upon, it is not unheard of that when confronting the other party each recognizes that serious damage can be done and the outcome is one in which a *pyrrhic* victory is all they can claim.

So what happens when both sides dig their heels in and refuse to relinquish any ground? What happens when we hit the unambiguous Mexican standoff phase of the battle? (For the record, Wikipedia defines *Mexican standoff* as "a confrontation between at least two parties in which neither party can proceed nor retreat without being exposed to danger. As a result, all participants need to maintain the strategic tension, which remains unresolved until some outside event makes it possible to resolve it.") Now, I am sure there are some who immediately make the false assumption that court is the only viable alternative, but it's not. Although ending up in court does happen on occasion, that occasion is rare, as it's expensive as well as time consuming. Nevertheless, attorneys enter the mix, establishing yet another weapon to be reckoned with.

Never make the false assumptions that lawyers are anxious to get into a courtroom; they're not, even if they're your own internal counsel. Whether a case is company against company, company against employee, employee against company, or any similar type of scenario, going to court creates a level of risk and uncertainty that most lawyers don't want to deal with, no matter which side of the table they sit on. Most lawyers are savvy enough to recognize that before ever hearing a case the court will insist on the parties going to arbitration, and of course arbitration, like everything else you do when you shoot back, costs money. This is obviously a greater concern when we have individuals taking on a company as opposed to company-against-company scenarios. Arbitration doesn't mean the threat of court doesn't exist, but it is a more palatable alternative when the parties involved are somewhat pliable. Depending on whether this is a company-on-company confrontation or a company-versus-employee confrontation, the outcome and the approach to it can be quite different.

By the time a company facing an individual goes to arbitration, it is virtually a given that the company is going to pay something. After all, why else would the individual be willing to accept the possibility? Any executive who thinks otherwise is naive. Many hardline executives will never go to arbitration because they understand there will be a payout attached. This may be a smart move if it can be substantiated—and I mean documented—that the action against the company is frivolous. In some instance, companies avoid the cost of arbitration by crafting programs designed to compensate contentious employees while demonstrating to them that should they get an attorney and go to arbitration, they could a smaller payout given the cost and potential risk of the arbitration process. Each case is different in nature, and thus going to arbitration will always be based on the nuances of the case. Arbitration is all about concessions when it involves an individual and a company, so the objective of the company is to use arbitration as a tool to mitigate their costs.

Individuals who enter arbitration need to go in open-minded and unemotional. Attempting to achieve some form of revenge in arbitration may prove to be more fatal to the individual than if he had just let himself take a bullet. The likelihood of being reinstated in your job, receiving a public apology, and reestablishing your integrity are things you will never recover in arbitration. An individual may have a "feel good" moment, but for the most part arbitration is never attended by the corporate people with whom the individual is most angry. So why as an individual go to arbitration seeking anything but financial compensation? An apology might be drawn out from the company during a session, but that apology may cost the individual in terms of what he ends up putting in his pocket. For the individual, arbitration does not mean you get everything you asked for; it is rather a negotiation to get as much of your "payola" as you can. In the words of Jerry Maguire, "Show me the money." Part of getting as much as you can means making sure you've brought plenty of ammunition—ammunition the company sees as a possible threat. A company going into arbitration will also bring its respective weapons of choice. These can include documents, e-mails, and statements from individuals or departments that suggest and justify the company's position. To give you an example, I was once deposed regarding a patent case where one of the defendants was a technology company I had worked for twelve years earlier. They pulled out an e-mail from me to someone in the company that said, "I agree," and they wanted to know what I meant by that. Are you kidding me? I could barely remember the name of the person I'd sent the e-mail to. If a company feels it has been falsely accused by an employee and has reached the arbitration table, then that company needs to load up with the ammunition necessary to make the employee believe the frivolity of her claims and cast significant doubt on whether the expense of moving forward will bring a satisfactory return.

When companies are at war with each other and have also reached that infamous Mexican standoff point that brings them to arbitration, the rules are significantly differently and the argument over who took the first shot quickly evaporates. Company-on-company gunfire that is brought to arbitration is totally dependent on what they're fighting about. If we are speaking about a takeover (whether a hostile or friendly acquisition but with points of contention), the situation will be subtly different from a merger, joint venture, or similar play. Companies in arbitration build substantial armies comprised of attorneys, finance people, business-specific people, top management, and possibly board members, depending on whether it is a public or private deal. These are the kind of sessions where people typically start off with the "Let's try and make this a win/win scenario for all the parties involved." A nanosecond after that comment is made, things typically degrade as each side stakes out its position. Thus, a standoff ensues. Despite the cost and the contentiousness of these situations, if the parties are willing, a transaction comes about (in which there is always a winner), and then the real shooting begins as departments, personnel, and products all come under fire relative to their need. If a settlement is not reached, then it may be time for the parties to throw down their weapons. In the case of most Mexican standoffs, both parties walk away from the table with pretty much what they went to the table with. Alternately, everyone pulls the trigger, and we know where that leaves us.

CHAPTER 29

THROW DOWN YOUR WEAPONS

*Fire the gun in the air and walk away; you
don't have to be a casualty in a war in which
you never intended to play a part*
—HARRY ROZAKIS

Whether the battleground is a company-on-company deal or an individual-on-company deal, there is a fairly simple way out for any of the parties to consider. There is no rule that says anyone has to shoot back in a contentious situation. Sometimes the best way to shoot back is to not shoot at all. It is mind-boggling that even at the corporate level you find businesses and individuals who insist on playing tit for tat, when the best course of action is to walk away. There are those who might see walking away as a fool's errand, particularly if there is a sense that the other party took the first shot. I like to think that sometimes having "thick skin" can lead to better results when shooting back than confronting the onslaught of something or someone who has you outgunned.

Although there are businesspeople who would argue that you can never separate yourself from your weapon, they would be significantly mistaken. They might ask, "How can laying your weapon down possibly be a good choice?" As we've said, shooting back is not without cost and is not without risk. Though there are individuals at both the management level and the employee level who like a good fight, most individuals on either side don't want to be engaged in protracted battles. This is not to say that some battles aren't exhilarating and challenging, particularly if they are skirmishes that can be resolved promptly, but protracted battles become exhausting, sometimes to the point where the parties can no longer stay fixated on what it was they were battling over. Ask most who have been in a protracted business battle, and they will tell you that even the winners don't relish the victory. The victory doesn't always justify the spoils.

If you're operating at a corporate level in a company-on-company battle, unless it is for the preservation of the company, you have to ask yourself if it's worth it to your business and what overall effect it may have. This assumes that preservation is good. Sometime bad companies try to make themselves believe self-preservation is good when in point of fact a sale or merger might really be the best solution for them. Does any executive really want to subject her people, time, and resources to an effort that has a minimum chance of coming to fruition, or where should it come to fruition, it becomes such a distraction for the company that its performance takes a hit? Either way, in these instances throwing down your weapons may be the best option for shooting back. What is one of the first things a hostage negotiator does? Puts down his weapons and says, "I'm not here to hurt you; we just want to work things out"? No, typically the hostage negotiator has all the firepower in the world behind him, but the reality is that shooting back probably isn't the best outcome for the hostages. On the corporate-to-corporate front, it is sometimes better to walk away than be embroiled in something that has no substantive conclusion. It saves all parties a great amount of money and mitigates potential negative exposure.

At the individual-to-company level, there may be more success in taking a Gandhi-like approach, at least initially. Revisiting the issues with the shooting party probably isn't going to get you rehired, but it may work in convincing them that perhaps a more favorable separation is in order and that the favorable separation might just prevent any unpleasantness down the road. From the company vantage point, not being "coldhearted bastards" can go a long way toward eliminating future headaches. During my career, whenever possible I always tried to provide the maximum separation package for employees unless there was a criminal or moral issue in play. I know there are many who may disagree, but in all my years I never had anyone come back and pursue legal action against the companies I ran. Allowing people to leave with a level of dignity goes a long way.

In those cases where the company is distressed, taking a position that allows you to explain the overall situation to the employees and confirming that you will maximize their benefits under the current cash limitations also makes employees feel that they are part of the process and not deadwood or being left as targets. On the employee side of this equation, you also have to understand the position of the company. This kind of occurrence is most often seen in start-ups. The majority of people recognize when they join a start-up that there is risk involved and the greatest is the company running out of capital. Over the years, I have seen the gamut, when it involves the venture capitalists who fund these failed start-ups. Some come in with guns blazing and leave a trail of bodies all around them, while other have dropped their weapons and stepped up and thanked the employees for their service and attempted to do their best to mitigate employee pain. When employees perceive that everything possible has been done to ease their hardship, weapons are laid down and people walk away.

On the corporate battlefield, throwing your guns down may not be the most recommended way of shooting back, but it should never be dismissed immediately. Like all forms of shooting back, planning is everything, and given that every situation takes on a life of its own, those shooting back need to realize that *any* type of shooting back, including throwing down your weapons, may be an option.

SECTION IV

Are You Dodging Bullets Or Shooting Back?

CHAPTER 30

EVERYBODY IS A SHOOTER

If someone has a gun and is trying to kill you, it would
be reasonable to shoot back with your own gun.
—*DALAI LAMA XIV*

I have attempted (hopefully with some success) to help you identify and profile the characteristics of the different kinds of shooters. It is easy, if one only reads this book superficially, to assume that I intended to demonize shooters and suggest they are somehow evil people. They're not! Given the dynamics of all business environments, you may in fact be a shooter, become a shooter, or, in the process of shooting back, take on the characteristics of one of the shooters I've described in this book. Shooters are a necessary force in business, particularly in troubled companies or with troublesome employees. Let's face it: not every company is a "great" company, and not every employee is a "stellar" performer. There are numerous instances of both companies and employees being guided back on course, but there are an equal number of instances where the company management or the employee(s) has to be changed. This is why it is so critical to ask the right questions. Asking critical questions before engaging shooters or becoming a shooter can be a real determination of what the outcome will be once the shots start being fired.

If you are the shooter or the party engaging the shooter, it's imperative you ask yourself questions from the perspective of those you are about to remove. Think about what those individuals will ask; go down the list of who, what, where, why, and when questions. These questions will be applicable whether you are taking out an individual or an entire division or even possibly an entire company. If you are unable to answer the questions before enlisting the efforts of the shooters, you are doing an injustice to the individual or individuals who have been targeted, an injustice to yourself, and more importantly an injustice to the company you represent. Throughout the course of this book, I have asked these questions in a number of different ways. What is the reason behind the action being taken? Why are these individuals being chosen? Who are the decision makers behind the actions being taken, and what justification do they have? How was the process for the action developed, and who owns the process? When was the decision actually made, and when will it be executed? If you're not constructing your questions in a format along these lines, then you'll be ill prepared for what might follow. Remember, the tougher the questions you ask before engaging the shooters, the better solutions you'll find and the more likely the action will move forward with minimal to no risk. As management or as a company, this line of Socratic questioning might just prevent you from having those you fire upon shoot back and in the process save you and your company a great deal of grief.

When shooters are engaged, the reasons are easily validated by those who engage them, but when those individuals act without applying intellect, the results are less than desirable. Most targets might challenge validating reasons, but very often those validating reasons are actually good reasons. The question is, can those executing the actions actually articulate them in a way that others understand? Of course, the acceptance of this reasoning is fully dependent on which end of the barrel you're standing.

Everybody is a shooter at one point or another during their career and for that matter in life. It would be very easy to take this concept of dodging bullets and shooting back into the realm of everyday life, but that's a book for someone else to write. There are shooters who develop because there are no more rocks to hide behind and they must shoot or die. Many shooters are reluctant or sometimes distraught over the task they must execute. Their task, however, may literally determine the very existence of a project, a department, or the company. In contrast, there are those shooters who truly relish their task. It is not uncommon, however, that these shooters will find they're subjected to the same tactics and actions they used to take out someone else. Then there are the folks who don't begin to grasp the fact that the activities they're engaged in are characteristically those of a shooter. Look around: I guarantee now that you're capable of identifying shooters and the act of shooting. You'll see more evidence of this in your workplace than you ever imagined.

Individuals become shooters because very often they are people capable of handling the task at hand. They rarely become one for malicious reasons, but rather because they are people who are capable of being extremely pragmatic in the way they approach things. Shooters have to be pragmatic, which also makes them accurate. Accuracy is critical because the repercussions of missing or wounding can create havoc for both those enlisting the shooter as well as the victim of the shooter. In more practical terms, it means that the cost goes up if the shooter is not accurate, even when the actual shooting is totally justified.

CHAPTER 31

AMMUNITION

*Great way to fight a war—be prepared
to defend yourself for winning.*
—CHRIS KYLE, AMERICAN SNIPER

The ammunition of business, politics, and life are the words that are spoken and the actions that are executed. All of these are more wounding and lethal than any hardware could ever be. Whether you are the shooter or the one shooting back, success is realized by those who have crafted the best story and implemented the most reliable actions. When a company wishes to move aggressively on an individual, group, or other corporation, its first recourse post planning is to load up on ammunition, and of course, the ammunition is predicated upon their planning. When a company or an individual wishes to mount a defense, they also load up on ammunition. The quality of the ammunition being used is always linked to the quality of the planning that's been done and ultimately impacts the result.

The metaphorical cannonball shot across the bow is nothing more than the first verbal or actionable sign that there may be a need to dodge a bullet. Similarly, that same bullet entering the heart is no less than an action that staggers or ends a professional career. It is all predicated on the shooter and the target. The most brutal and callous form of this are two words that have been around for a long time but became associated with Donald Trump as a result of his show *The Apprentice*: "You're fired!" Most company HR departments have realized that the Trump style is great for TV but not really effective in the litigious environment we now live and work in. Whether or not the action is justified or not, the politically correct police have gotten legal departments and HR departments convinced that the words "you're fired" are disparaging. As a result, most bosses today are politically correct and socially polite. Terminations these days sound more like, "Sorry, Mary, but we no longer require your services," or "Hey, Frank, it appears you've outgrown your position and it's time to move on," or "Hey, sales team, the company is restructuring and, well, the way we sell will be changing." Hmmm, sounds like "you're fired" to me, and only the naive don't see it for what it is. Nevertheless, these words very often seem to disarm the individual for the moment, avoid immediate confrontation, and convince the legal and HR teams that they've "dodged a bullet."

If you're the shooter and you shoot one across the bow, you're providing the target the opportunity to dodge a bullet by affording him or her ample warning about what's coming next. It might be all that's necessary to prompt the individual to take action, which is in his or her own best interest and in the interest of the company. Essentially, to leave. The ammunition being fired here include phrases like: "Looks like our new management may be evaluating personnel in your department," or "It seems like your talents go beyond the ability of the company to compensate you long term," or "Wouldn't a change of direction in your career be good for your personal growth?" Give me a break! A decision concerning whether or not to leave will most often be linked to the money tied to leaving. If the individual gets a great compensation package and it is reasonable, there are no hard feelings. "Reasonable," however, is at times difficult to pin down. If an individual believes she will be terminated without compensation but with justifiable cause, she may just choose to leave. I have had employees who have been reprimanded for some action they've engaged in or because of a failure to perform and have simply said, "If you come down to my office again with respect to this issue, it will be to submit your resignation." I have been very fortunate that this has worked effectively. However, when an individual believes there is not satisfactory compensation or justification, that's when the shooting back begins, and you'd better be loading up on ammunition. If you've gotten that shot across the bow, as a target with any foresight at all you realize your "ass" has been saved this time around, and planning your next steps become critical. One way or another, you will find yourself either prepping your ammunition or packing up your bags.

When you've taken a direct hit and lose your job, your salary, your colleagues, and in some cases even your family, life as you know it has reached a lot more than a strategic inflection point. If you're the recipient of an unwanted bullet, it can be the most disarming event in your life. There is usually little time to assess how much ammunition you have to fight back. The worst thing you can do is have a knee-jerk reaction, whether verbal or through some kind of foolish action. Given that you now have all the time in the world, it is better to think through your next move. Why telegraph what you're going to do next and allow the other side to build up their own ammunition reserves? Why not stealthily create the perception that you understand and recognize that these things happen. Being responsive should always be done on your time line and under your terms and conditions, and *only* after you make sure you are truly able to shoot back.

Of course, if you're the one who made the fatal shot, then mission accomplished! So the question here is, is there such a thing in business and in politics as a justifiable kill? Once again, the answer is, absolutely! Provided the right target has been hit, of course. Did you preserve ammo? Did you use up all your ammo? Is the ammo you have enough to do the job? How much ammo does the other guy have? These are all questions to be asked prior to any shot being fired. Ammunition in this instance is all the backup data you have to ensure that the actions taken were supportable. It is also the words that were chosen to be fired from your mouth when finally pulling the trigger. When you're a shooter, the words you use can make all the difference in terms of the target's ability to dodge a bullet and shoot back.

CHAPTER 32

SURVIVAL AND RESURRECTION

Survival was my only hope, success my only revenge.
—PATRICIA CORNWELL

There is always a war waging somewhere, and as I've suggested multiple times in this book, the business world is no different. But not all targets go on to live a life of loss, victimization, despair, and sorrow. No matter how challenging the struggle is, there is an outcome that leads to renewal, optimism, and success. Shootouts should not be seen pessimistically, as though there is a big bad world where the axiom "kill or be killed" applies. It may seem this way if you're a nihilist, but then, nihilists don't belong in business. Business is about survival and success while exceeding the expectations of others and yourself. For those who will reach for it, the business world not only offers redemption but it also allows for a metamorphosis of character and experience. Having your business closed, being terminated or passed over for a position, and seeing your company fail or be acquired can all be devastating if allowed. At the same time, it can also force the transition that a person or company would not have taken without the impetus, and that change just might prove to be exactly what was needed.

There are no guarantees you can win or survive every gunfight, but you can resurrect yourself to fight another day, and fight with a wisdom you didn't have or didn't know you had before. The wounds of the battle do cut deep, but they will heal provided you never give up. This is sometimes easier said than done, but the narrative is real. I speak as someone who has been on both ends of the barrel, and in either instance, I've come out all the better for it. These experiences have always resulted in my learning more about being better in business and better as a person. I have never known failure, but I have experience not succeeding. You can't fail if you refuse to quit; you can only take what you've learned and do it better the next time.

Fortunately, the business world is like the universe, filled with an array of habitable and uninhabitable planets. These planets offer the opportunity for redemption and resurrection when people are prepared to dust themselves off, reenter a new battle, and be engaged. History has its value as a record of things past and as a provider of new tools for your arsenal, but history does not dictate what will occur in the future unless you choose to let it.

The winners in this universe don't spend their careers dodging bullets; they learn how not to have to dodge them in the first place. Whether shooting or shooting back, those who are successful at it don't shoot first and ask questions later. They ask the right questions first, and should they shoot, they shoot with deadly accuracy. Preparation and knowledge are everything when it comes to dodging bullets and shooting back.

EPILOGUE

Incidences of dodging bullets and shooting back are more than a little common in business and in life, and I have little doubt that you, the reader of this book, not only related to some of the scenarios described but in fact have been on one end of the gun or the other. I also feel confident that over the course of your life or career, you either have or will become a shooter or encounter one of the shooters I've detailed. In some cases, the shooter may be exactly as I've described or an individual who is a composite of two or more of the profiled shooters. If you haven't become a shooter or confronted one yet in your life, then you've yet to fire or been shot the metaphoric bullet. If this is the case, then you should consider yourself to be a lot of things, but lucky isn't one of them. A time will come when your only alternative is to be a shooter or the target. Occasionally, I've come across that rare individual who has been shot so many times that he or she has been unable to identify being shot for what it is and as a result lives a life and has a career that is always in turmoil. Don't ever let yourself become one of these people. You may not like being on the wrong end of the barrel, but at least you will know where you stand.

Although I've attempted to capture the world of dodging bullets and shooting back through the various examples in the book, there are situations where a bullet fired in your direction is impossible to dodge and can become among the biggest challenge of your life. These are situations where the shooter becomes life itself, and where all the preparation in the world could have never prevented you from being on the receiving end. In these situations, it is not about preparation but all about how you respond and fire back. I'd like to provide two such examples:

As far back as my late teens and early twenties, despite being an extremely active in an array of sports and workout routines, I always suffered from what many tried to call sports-induced asthma and what some physicians described as a form of stress. Despite visiting with a multitude of doctors over the next twenty years, nothing really changed except that my ability to breathe became more and more difficult. By the age of forty, my family and I had lived and traveled throughout the world, I had a successful career, and I owned my own tech company. By this point in my life, I had become accustomed to dodging bullets and shooting back in all aspects of my career, and I wouldn't be honest if I didn't say there were many instances when I was doing the shooting. Like all individuals, I had my share of learning experiences (failure has never been an option), but I also had some great victories. My attitude toward life has always been: "Take your best shot." And then life gave me what I had threatened it to do.

In an effort to address what had been a nagging breathing problem that was getting worse, I went to Stanford University Medical Center to see a pulmonary specialist. After they ran a gamut of tests, I met with the doctor only to hear him say, "It's a good thing you came to see us today, Mr. Rozakis, because in one to two years you'll either be dead or in the heart-lung transplant clinic." I had developed something called chronic thrombo-embolic pulmonary hypertension (CTEPH), which is essentially the blocking of your pulmonary arteries by emboli that attach themselves to the pulmonary arteries and form scar tissue, cutting off the supply of oxygen to the heart. Life had fired a bullet at me that had been lodged in my body and had gone misdiagnosed for almost twenty-plus years. It was something I could have neither predicted nor prevented.

After quite a bit of deliberation with my family, I realized there was only one thing for me to do and that was to shoot back by putting together the strongest posse I could muster. There is no cure for primary pulmonary hypertension (PH), and the life expectancy for a PH patient is typically only a few to several years. In 1993 when I was finally diagnosed, there were no known therapies and the only possible option for a patient with my form of the disease was a rare surgery being performed at University of California San Diego Medical Center. Patients had to be candidates for the surgery, and the reality was that most people weren't. My posse, which was now the medical professionals at Stanford and UCSD, went into action to see what they could do for me. It was determined I was a candidate for a pulmonary thrombo-endarterectomy (PTE), a form of heart bypass surgery during which your pulmonary arteries are essentially rotor-rootered. I was to be the 495th person to ever have the surgery. The fact that I am here to write this book today is a credit to the posse that formed around me and those who made shooting back a possibility. As one might imagine, surviving a situation like this did not make me invincible, but I can tell you it eliminated any fears I would have in the future about bullets that could be fired upon me in a business environment.

I believe my brush with death prepared me for another dodging-bullets-and-shooting-back event, which emerged from a place I couldn't possibly have considered. It was 2003, and I was CEO of a NASDAQ-listed technology company headquartered in Hong Kong. At the time my team and I thought the biggest challenge facing us was driving sales and improving our share price. I was brought in to manage the turnaround of a company that had seen a dramatic reduction in sales and its share price. What my team and I were not prepared for was something taking aim at us from the shadows, which was something that few CEOs have ever or will ever have to face. Like something out of the Bible or some mythical story, the SARS epidemic descended upon Hong Kong and our company with unrelenting speed, and literally changed our priorities from our business to the lives of our people. Panic set in unbelievably fast, and a bustling city of six million plus became a near ghost town. Customers from around the world were asking us if it was safe to receive shipments and correspondence because of the perceived potential of contamination. Our workforce of almost two thousand was afraid and perplexed. Instead of dealing with clients, accountants, and attorneys, I was now dealing with doctors, government health departments, and pharmaceutical supply companies. Our business was under attack, but by something we could have never imagined. Dodging bullets now involved protecting the health of our employees. Wearing masks, wearing gloves, and the daily temperature taking of our employees (from the janitors to the CEO's office) became our new way of operating. The eeriness of the situation was something out of a science fiction movie. We had an enemy on whom we could not return fire, and we could only dodge what it threw at us with the tools the medical and safety community recommended. As a company, we dodged a number of bullets during that period, and we survived the hell that had been brought down upon us almost unscathed. The same was not true for a few family members of our employees who were not so fortunate. Living, let alone managing, through an experience like this is something you can never learn in any business school or from any book.

I have learned a great deal throughout my career about dodging bullets and shooting back, and I carry the battle scars to prove it. I have seen some of the bullets being fired, and like the two aforementioned stories indicated, I have been blindsided at times by things that seemed incomprehensible. Every bullet I've dodged and even the few that have hit me have been an incredible learning experience. The bullets will always keep flying, sometimes at you and sometimes around you. When you're a shooter, be quick and efficient, and make sure you've considered the consequences of your actions. If you get hit, you need to understand that all wounds can heal if you let them, and once they have, you must keep moving forward.

www.ingramcontent.com/pod-product-compliance
Lightning Source LLC
Chambersburg PA
CBHW072304200526
45168CB00014B/453